T0130222

WHAT GOD DOES NOT KNOW

What God Does Not Know

A Layman Looks At The Parable Of the Prodigal Son

Roger R. Dubois

WestBow Press

A DIVISION OF THOMAS NELSON
& ZONDERVAN

WestBow Press books may be ordered through booksellers or by contacting:

WestBow Press
A Division of Thomas Nelson & Zondervan
1663 Liberty Drive
Bloomington, IN 47403
www.westbowpress.com
1 (866) 928-1240

THE HOLY BIBLE, NEW INTERNATIONAL VERSION®,
NIV® Copyright © 1973, 1978, 1984, 2011 by Biblica, Inc.®
Used by permission. All rights reserved worldwide.

ISBN: 978-1-9736-6870-1 (sc)
ISBN: 978-1-9736-6872-5 (hc)
ISBN: 978-1-9736-6871-8 (e)

Library of Congress Control Number: 2019909046

Print information available on the last page.

WestBow Press rev. date: 8/22/2019

DEDICATION

Dedicated to all the prodigals I've walked with throughout my journey. May you experience all that God does not know.

DEDICATION

Dedicated to all the prodigals I've walked with throughout my journey. May you experience all that God does not know.

"The Prodigal Son is a story that speaks about love that existed before any rejection was possible and will still be there after all rejections have taken place."

HENRI NOUWEN

"The Prodigal Son is a story that speaks about love that existed before any rejection was possible and will still be there after all rejections have taken place."

HENRI NOUWEN

CHAPTER ONE
THE REALIZATION

I was dead and I didn't know it.

I'd been walking around for years breathing. Inhaling and exhaling as if it was completely normal for the dead to use oxygen.

I wore the finest hand-made clothes, purchased from the best shops in the city. My clothes weren't off-the rack or cheap imports. They were hand-made by skilled craftsman. What was not tailor-made was imported from the finest clothing manufacturers across the globe. You wouldn't find a store-bought shirt with a "Made in China" tag in my closet. If I passed you on the street, you could say I was the best dressed dead man you had ever seen.

I was not only fashionably dressed, but also impeccably groomed. I spared no expense for my weekly haircut, manicure, and pedicure. I didn't merely have a barber, I had a "personal grooming assistant". With every hair trimmed and in place, I was the illustration of what a fashionable man with means should look like. Apart from being dead, I thought I looked fantastic. I had no doubt, I was the best dressed and finest looking corpse in the city. I just didn't know it.

My car was the definition of luxury on four wheels. Even those who thought they were successful were jealous. They were jealous because they believed a young man, like me, couldn't or shouldn't be able to afford such a car. They envied the leather interior, premium sound system, custom wheels, and reflective, black metallic paint. I chuckled when they would drool gazing at my car. What they didn't know was I was driving my own hearse. Who knew dead men could drive?

I never had to wait to be seated at the finest restaurants where I was known by name. It was so satisfying to walk past the line of people waiting for a table.

Before I became wealthy, I went to lunch with my father at a low-budget café. At this café, just before the swinging door that led the servers into and out of the kitchen hundreds of times in a day, was an amusing sign. It said:

'If you die while at work please fall over, it is the only way to tell the difference.'

Since we didn't eat out often, I considered it a treat before I realized the finest restaurants served dead customers too. What irony. I was a dead person laughing at a sign about dead people falling over so other dead people would know they were actually dead. The problem was, even then, I just didn't know I was dead. I didn't have the common sense to fall over.

I spent years living in luxury, spending my wealth without care or a thought for tomorrow. I thought I was really living, but I was deceived. I was dead and completely clueless about that fact.

All my friends were dead too. We were out celebrating every vice night after night. If anyone asked, we'd say we were living the dream, life as it was meant to be when actually the dream was an illusion, a nightmare in which we weren't really living. We surrounded ourselves with like-minded dead people who looked and behaved just like we did.

We didn't realize the life was a lie, a thin veil that covered our eyes. We were living life to its fullest, but the truth was we were all dead.

To be honest, I want to point out that most of the time I didn't want to know the reality of my condition. Seriously, who wants to admit they're a walking and talking dead person? An animated corpse you could say. The truth of my condition knocked on my door more than once, but I either couldn't or wouldn't comprehend it. I was blind to my true condition.

The truth knocked when a friend suddenly died after a night out on the town. His death hit us hard. All of his friends cried at his funeral and offered condolences to his family. The minister brought some comfort, but he lost me when he said all of us are facing the same problem with the same result. We comforted each other with a pat on the back, a shoulder to cry on, and another round of drinks. With our glasses raised high, we saluted our friend with a toast. The truth knocked, but I wouldn't answer.

Reality knocked again when one of our group found "religion." He tried to tell us of the change he experienced, but we shunned him. He was one of my best friends and I ignored what he was saying.

One day he invited me to lunch. We met at one of the finest establishments in the city and over the next two hours he expressed the change in his life and invited me to "Come alive and see what I was missing."

"That may work for you and I'm glad you're happy, but that isn't for me." I told him.

When he pressed the subject, I grew angry and pushed back verbally. Suddenly, I realized this guy, one of my closest friends, was now completely different. I felt uneasy and empty but didn't know why. One thing was for sure, I was no longer hungry for conversation. After I ended lunch, we shook hands and I never saw him again. The truth called but I wouldn't hear.

Although most of the time I didn't want to acknowledge my condition, there were those moments I knew something was wrong. When you walk into a room but can't recall why you're there, you pause, shrug, and leave empty-handed. Or, you feel the heat of the first hot summer day and a cool breeze sparks a memory you can't quite place. The memory teases, but when you try to focus, it turns to vapor leaving you sad. Or, when seeing a piece of furniture calls you back to a time in your life filled with love and joy, before the pain of life stole your innocence and your dreams. For that brief few seconds you recall the truth of love. You want to reach out and grasp it, but your arms remain empty and you realize you are too.

The truth is nearly everyone around us is dead. Like me, they don't know it. It's hard to share that fact. As soon as you inform someone they may, in fact, be dead they tend to write you off. Just as I did when I had lunch with my friend, I rejected what would give me life. But, when one person listens and hears the truth of their situation, the potential for life, real life, suddenly leaps into view.

You can call me Jim. This is my story. In the pages that follow, I'll introduce myself and many of you will realize that my story is as old as humanity. This may be your story as well. Of course, some of the details are different; different times, different places, or even different circumstances. But our stories are similar. You might be able to finish my story before the end of the chapter. Our story has been repeated countless times over the centuries. Just like me, many of you were dead and, just like me, you found life.

Others are also just like me, when I was dead. It's okay, go ahead and chuckle. If you're in the same condition, you're a dead person reading a book that opens with a dead man telling his story. It does seem strange, but we were dead to the truth of life. You'll say the same things I did. 'I'm a good person.' 'I believe in God.' 'I went to church.' 'My family is very religious.' And the list of phrases could go on. Yes, you are just like me.

As my story unfolds, you'll also hear about spiritual truths that brought knowledge of my death to my attention. You may say when I realized how completely dead I was, it had my full attention. And, when the Truth had my undivided attention, then I experienced redemption. Life, real life, followed and changed everything. It's often said, Jesus is the answer, but is that true? Is there something, anything that God does not know? Is it possible that one answer could not only satisfy all other questions but also meet the deepest desire in your heart?

Chapter Two

Is This All There Is?

I s this all there is? How many times have you asked yourself that question? Shouldn't there be more to life?

In my senior year of high school, life was unfolding. Graduating is one of life's biggest "freedom" moments. You stand at the door of your future. For most of us, up to this point, life wasn't under our control. Where we lived, went to school, or what we did was all dictated by someone else. But, graduation offers wide-ranging options, the world is suddenly wide open.

My post-graduation plans were not much different from many of yours. These included attending college, getting a job, and having a career. But, all that had to wait, I was going on a celebratory road trip. My buddy Jimmy and I had planned this trip for nearly a year. We traveled from Rhode Island to the West. We visited Yellowstone, Hoover Dam, Las Vegas, and the Grand Canyon. We slept under the stars on the shores of the Great Lakes, rode dirt bikes through the mountains of central Idaho, and fished the Snake River. We traveled due west, then south to

Arizona, then across the South through Mississippi and Georgia before heading north to West Virginia, Ohio and home. The car Jimmy and I drove on our road trip broke down often. We spent two weeks in West Unity, Ohio repairing the car, replaced a cracked head in Illinois, and spent days in Nampa, Idaho fixing the cooling system. Nearly five months after starting our tour Jimmy and I pulled into my parent's driveway. It had been a challenging but exciting trip. At no other time in my life have I had the freedom to do something so carefree.

A new car would have been an excellent solution to all these breakdowns. However, I have a memory from that same time that isn't as pleasant. A father, at another Rhode Island high school, gave his son a new car for a graduation present. I didn't know this young man, but I imagine when his father handed him the car keys he was overjoyed. On the threshold of his life, a week or two before graduation, this young man and two or three of his buddies were killed in a collision with a semi-truck. Suddenly there was only pain and suffering. We were the same age. I was undoubtedly just as rambunctious as they were. But they never graduated, never traveled across the United States, or experienced everything available to young men just entering the prime of life. There was no more for them. You have to ask, "Is this all there is?"

Even worse, this isn't an isolated case. These tragic events happen all over the world to some of the most innocent people. Over the years I've been touched by personal tragedies everywhere I've lived. A young child is killed crossing the street. A young mother is diagnosed with stage four cancer. A military member is grievously injured in a training accident. A young father goes to the gym to play a little basketball, collapses, and dies of a heart attack before medical help arrives. A fifteen-year-old tries an unknown drug for the first time and never lives to see sweet sixteen. There was no more for them. Many never have the chance to discover the truth that there is truly more to life.

Is this all there is? Shouldn't there be more to life?

The question isn't only asked when we're faced with the finality of death. The daily grind of life is enough to create it. A partner who promised life-long commitment comes home one day and says, "I quit." There's never enough in the checking account. The kids outgrow the jeans you purchased last month. You work endlessly, but never seem to get ahead. There's an old saying, "When you work your fingers to the bone, what do you get? Boney fingers." Ecclesiastes 2:17 states, "So I hated life, because the work that is done under the sun was grievous to me. All of it is meaningless, a chasing after the wind." This is the weariness of life. As day drags into day and beats us down you ask, "Is this all there is? Is this all I have to look forward to?"

Many years ago, I volunteered at a Christian coffee house named "The Lighthouse." In the 1980's, these types of places served as an outreach ministry, typically in an area with bars, bars, and more bars. The Lighthouse was similar to many others around the country. It had a simple store front with two fifteen-foot glass windows. One window was painted with a large lighthouse, its wide yellow beam scanning the shoreline and illuminating the ocean as waves crashed over jagged rocks. The glass front door, centered between the two windows, simply stated "The Lighthouse." We were open most evenings during the week as well as every weekend. Our small group of believers held weekly Bible studies and nightly fellowship. One of our major attractions was food and, when we could, bands that played contemporary Christian music.

With no cover charge, free food, and music, people were always popping in to see what we were about. Although I met many people at the myriad of events during that period, there is one person I remember as if it was yesterday.

This quiet night was unusual because there was no music and very little food. Even though I don't remember his name, I can still see this man as he walked in through the front door. He was nearly six feet tall and muscular with a Mohawk haircut. He had a dark tan. Although his clothes were clean, he had a distinct odor. He looked lost and clearly didn't understand that we were just Christians hanging out and drinking coffee.

After I introduced myself he asked, "What is this place?" I explained we were a Christian coffee house where groups got together and talked about the Lord. This concept seemed foreign to him. But, as we continued to talk, I shared the Gospel, answered his questions about God, and what it meant to accept Jesus as his Savior. I thought we were having an interesting conversation and wanted to introduce him to some of the others. I placed my hand on his shoulder and indicated for him to follow me.

He quickly said, "Wait, you can't put your arm on me." When I asked why not, he replied, "Because I'm a sheepherder and I smell."

I wasn't raised around sheep, but I assumed both of those things were true. I once hauled hay to a sheep camp in Idaho with my grandfather. I also went to an agricultural school in Lincoln, Rhode Island. Working around animals comes with a certain difficult-to-escape aroma. This young man couldn't escape from his profession nor the smell associated with it. He wasn't repulsive to me or the others at The Lighthouse, but to himself, he was. If anyone got close, he would react by throwing up a defensive shield to warn them off. His shield said, "Don't get too close, I'm a sheepherder and I stink."

After talking for another hour, as he left I invited him back.

He returned several nights later. He had just come in from the field and the odor was even stronger. We talked until it was closing time.

Normally, I walked to my nearby apartment. As we closed and locked the front door, my sheepherder friend offered me a ride. "Hey," I told him. "That's great. You can come up and meet my roommates. They're Christians and we have Bible studies in our apartment. You can join us." Suddenly, that wall was raised again.

"I can't go into your apartment," he exclaimed.

"Of course, you can. It'll be great. My friends would like to meet you." was my response.

"No, I can't. Don't you remember? I'm a sheepherder and I stink," he sadly reminded me.

"You can still come into my apartment. Of course, you can. Please come meet my friends. They'll make you feel welcome," I pressed. We drove to the apartment, but he refused to get out of the car and I couldn't convince him to join us. I showed him which apartment and told him to come anytime. Sadly, I never saw him again.

Clearly, the life my sheepherder friend lived stigmatized him especially in his own mind far more than it did to others. If your chosen profession identifies you as worthy or unworthy, is this all there is?

If you've ever leaned over the hospital bed of a loved one fighting for life, do you ask, "Is this all there is?" Does life deal the cards and what you receive determines what you can expect? Do you have the right to expect more than what life deals out?

The way many of us label success is wrong. There are those who appear to have everything, but still struggle with life's questions. Having "it all" doesn't necessarily mean you will "have it all."

I've lived and traveled in many parts of the globe and talked with people of different cultures and beliefs. No matter where we're from, the religion that shaped our country or family heritage, or what our cultural background, the questions are the same. I've discovered in conversations that all groups have strikingly similar concerns. If you ever had opportunities to talk one-on-one with someone searching for answers or with deeply personal questions, you would again find very similar inquires.

The following chapters discuss four spiritual truths I believe every person needs to know. I'll introduce you to people who had real questions, who needed authentic answers, and who had a genuine life struggle. These truths provide foundations we can build upon.

CHAPTER THREE
THE STRUGGLE IS REAL.

The struggle is real.

In the first chapter, we were introduced to Jim. Before we venture further, let me pause and submit a brief disclaimer. Although we're going to take a close look at Jim, we should realize he's fictional. Jim isn't real. However, as we get to know him better, I hope we see ourselves in his attitudes, his personality, and in his dreams and longings for a different future. Hopefully, we'll be able to see how we all seek a better life and to find answers to issues that swirl around us. I also anticipate we'll recognize the parts of his story we aren't happy about in our own. We all struggle with anger and feel vulnerable because of our weaknesses, the habits and sins that create chaos, and the regrets we leave behind. Jim may not be real, but I hope we can see there's some of him in all of us.

In chapter one, Jim describes the realization that he was physically alive but spiritually dead. Physically he seemed fine, but in reality, he was as dead as a door knob. Like the rest of us, as Jim grew up he endeavored to find what his life was meant to be. Over and over he asked what his life's purpose was. Why was he here? Was he loved? Was there something more?

We all question why we are on this earth. I've been asked by teenagers, by young adults, and by folks who find their house empty when the last child leaves to start their own life. I've even been asked by the elderly in their twilight years, "What is life's purpose?" It's a hard question. One of the biggest questions you'll ever ask yourself. I've met people who found their purpose. Of course, I've also met others who never did. But, I believe there is one far more important question, and that's our deep-seated need for acceptance. As a matter of fact, I believe it's one question everyone asks at some point in their life and we all seek to know the answer.

Although Jim is our main character, we're going to take a look at the Jim in each of us. If Jim is indeed like all of us, then his struggles and questions are no different from our struggles and questions today. Most of the others we'll meet as the pages of this book unfold have similar conflicts. They each wrestled with various questions, just as you and I do. However, I want to focus on one particular question we face at one time or another. Many of us may deny this ordeal exists. Whether we ever think about it, try to answer the nagging questions, or verbally or silently deny the questions are within us, I believe we share a similar story. Each of us could share the equivalent tale, even those who refuse to acknowledge it.

We all struggle for acceptance. The question we seek answers for is: are we accepted for who we really are? It's larger than how we feel or think we are accepted into our place in the world. At some point, we feel we don't belong. Even in non-exclusive groups some don't feel they fit in. Some are in very exclusive groups until the group decides they don't belong. Even when we rise to the top of the corporate structure, the distressing sense that something is missing, that ultimately we are not accepted, can be very difficult to deal with. We search for a sense of belonging. We react to being ostracized from the group.

Looking back at Jim, if the subject came up, I imagine he'd shrug his shoulders. Maybe he'd make light of the seriousness of it and pass it off as not a big deal. It's possible Jim's friends learned it was best not to broach the subject very often. The point is that people react differently to spiritual questions. Some with an angry outburst. Some with a comical, philosophical response.

Paul, a friend of mine, took this approach. Paul and I were with a group of friends discussing various spiritual issues. Paul brought the debate to a stop with his philosophical "mayonnaise jar" response.

"I think our little world is inside an empty mayonnaise jar," he said. "This mayonnaise jar is kept in some guy's closet on a shelf where he keeps other worlds in other empty mayonnaise jars. Every so often, he takes our jar off the shelf and looks at us, then puts us back on the shelf with the other mayonnaise jars."

It took me a long time to realize that maybe, just maybe, this was Paul's way of avoiding the conflict within himself. Putting hard-hitting questions in storage and out of sight is one way of ignoring them. Paul put his questions in that proverbial mayonnaise jar, stored it on a closet shelf, and forgot about it. Of course, there are others who deal with the battle of our acceptance in other ways.

For a few of us, the fight is painful and it wars against our soul. It's too much to face and we can't come to grips with it, but neither can we let it go. The heartache becomes turmoil and the turmoil within often creates chaos in every aspect of our lives.

The event that brought the struggle to the forefront won't end. We relive the memory and pain repeatedly and it dictates our responses. Or, although we can't remember a particular triggering event, it refuses to release the grip it has on our mind, spirit, and soul. The struggle is real, never ending, and full of anguish.

For some, the acceptance question is merely a nagging thought that crops up from time to time, but it doesn't rule us. We hardly ever think about it until it rises to the surface, where we seek answers in a variety of ways, until it sinks back into the hidden rooms of our heart. It reminds us of a childhood memory we can't seem to recall. We may dwell on it for a few moments, but it's like trying to catch a handful of fog. When the question does cross our minds, we try to find the answers but then decide to simply move on and focus our attention elsewhere until the next time it decides to resurface.

I once had a conversation with an elderly man in the airport as we waited for our flight. He was inquisitive about spiritual matters. He said he read a wide variety of books and asked questions over the years, always searching but never really finding the answers to those questions continuously circling in his mind.

Some acknowledge the conflict, but because the answers aren't apparent, they set it aside without a second thought. When a spiritual matter is discussed, there's often an unexplained tension. This tension may build into a surprising outburst that shocks those around us and often the resulting eruption is ignored but it effectively ends the conversation. We face the questions with a certain level of animosity that isn't logical. I once knew a man who, if you mentioned God or asked a question about a spiritual issue, would state he didn't believe such things and refused to participate in any discussion. However, if the dialogue continued without him, he would grow more verbally aggressive and would become upset about something he claimed he didn't believe. Once he became physically violent by slamming his hands on the table, then stood up, pointed his finger at each of us, and threatened anyone who continued the conversation. His battle for acceptance was real but he wouldn't acknowledge it.

In each category I mentioned are a host of other individuals who deal with this same struggle in differing degrees. Some of us see our world through the eyes of this struggle. It impacts all we do and is never far from us. For others, it clouds our vision of not only ourselves but also how we think others see us. The struggle for acceptance doesn't always diminish when we achieve success. Success sometimes lessens the trial, but often makes it worse. Discussing our endeavor to feel and know acceptance while in a group helps some, while others find group work more difficult. We seldom freely share this battle with others.

Being surrounded by friends doesn't make our struggle disappear, but often intensifies it instead. You would think the conflict would stop when you're in the company of the few people who really love and accept you. Of course, there are those friends who actually reduce the internal battle. Sometimes their love compels you to lay the struggle aside and be the best you can. However, our quest for answers is complicated and we always pick it back up. Others keep searching for answers to questions they don't know. That nagging question in the back of your mind. Others conclude the answers will never come. They shrug their shoulders and live and let live. Is it possible that throughout history every human being has had this struggle? Some may think they've won. Meanwhile, many others think they've contained it in a mental box where they lock it away. Sadly, some of us feel we will never win and others just don't care anymore.

When my children were small my wife and I attempted to

plug them into clubs, groups, and sports to get them engaged with other children, learn new skills, and have fun. In order to protect their fragile self-esteem, no scores were kept at sporting events and they were encouraged by being told, "GREAT GAME!" at the end of each contest. The coaches also gave everyone participation trophies at the end of the season. It didn't matter how many games they actually won or lost. It was supposed to give them a good self-image, make them feel good about themselves. My daughter was in dance, cheerleading, basketball, t-ball, softball, and other groups through her teenage years. We put my son into Scouts, soccer, basketball, t-ball, and baseball. My wife and I provided a loving home, went to all their games and performances, and made sure they felt good about their accomplishments. To ensure we had quality time with each child, I took time away from work, signed each one out of school at least once a month, and took them to lunch. My wife gave them both special time with her. Each child was given undivided attention to convey our love and acceptance. I followed suggestions from "experts" to ensure they each knew how much they were loved.

Despite both children being fully engaged in activities throughout the years, and spending quality, as well as quantity time with both parents, neither child entered their teenage or adult years with an intact positive self-image. Both my son and daughter wrote personal letters questioning why they felt less important than the other. This confused my wife and me. In spite of all our efforts, they each struggled with acceptance.

I've been successful in my chosen career. I worked extremely hard throughout my time in the military, achieved the highest enlisted rank, and had a stellar reputation. At every professional military education course I attended, I achieved some of the highest awards at graduation. I went through college, earning a

Master of Business Administration degree with excellent grades. Still, during those times of success as well as the difficult times many young adults face, I struggled with feeling accepted.

At one point, I made a conscious effort to build a facade which reflected what I wanted people to see, who I wanted people to think I was. That is what a reputation is, isn't it? Isn't it what people think you are, the reflection of who you portray, not necessarily who you really are? A reputation, that isn't based on who you really are can ultimately be a house-of-cards. You work to build this magnificent structure but it's shaky and tumbles down with the slightest breeze or a poorly placed card. This is what happened to our friend Jim, which we'll see in the coming chapters.

When I talk to people who haven't come to a place in life where they've come alive, I'm reminded of my own trial. Even though "I know Whom I have believed" (2 Timothy 1:12) and know He accepts me just as I am, I never want to forget the fight I had with this whole idea of acceptance.

Recently, I was listening to a minister tell the story of a woman who didn't know her biological father. She was 23 years old when she began a search for her father; a search with some significant challenges. She didn't know his name. She only knew he and her mother met in a particular Canadian city. She took out an ad in that city's newspaper listing her mother's name and requesting her father contact her. The ad provided information on how to verify he was her father, as well as how to contact her. Her ad subsequently caught a reporter's eye and he asked to do a human-interest story. She accepted the opportunity because it would certainly help her quest. After a few questions, the reporter asked his most obvious one, "Why? If you haven't known your biological father all this time, why are you searching now?"

The woman's response was simple, "Because something is missing in my life and I want to fill that missing part."

To varying degrees, we're all in search of the missing part. We're searching for where we come from, where we belong, and the reason we are here in the first place. We want to know that our father, the one who created us, knows and accepts us. If it's important to know our biological father, how much more do these questions call to our soul for answers to our spiritual existence?

This book is about acceptance. We're going to look at how one person, Jim, searched for acceptance and how his desperate search nearly destroyed his life, but never provided the answers his heart required. We'll also discover that when he gave up his search, he finally found acceptance in the one place he least expected. That discovery made all the difference.

I'm going to touch on many aspects of acceptance. To some degree we all have to deal with how we address this issue. We can ignore, deny, or try to deal with the issue. We can vehemently fight against it. Some are able to reach the place where it's not a significant issue. Just as the young woman did, we can search for the answers to the questions with our whole being. However, there's only one way to ultimately find the acceptance we seek.

Before we go any further, I need to provide some clarification. I'm a layman. I'm not an ordained minister or a member of the clergy. I haven't attended Bible school or seminary, nor have I had any special church or denominational training. However, I do believe I am called by God to minister. I'm a layman who has experienced the most important acceptance I know.

From the start of my faith journey, when I first came to the foot of the Cross, I've been accepted. Songs of acceptance capture my heart. DeGarmo and Key, a contemporary Christian music group from the 1980's and 1990's, performed songs that resonated with me when I was younger and still grab my attention all these years later. One song, "All the Losers Win," speaks to "losers, who lose all guilt and sin." [2] Anyone who considers themselves a loser, knows the desire they have for acceptance.

Another song by the same group addresses the facet of acceptance that's not related to success. As I mentioned earlier, success does not provide the answer. I've known many successful people who questioned their own place in the world. We've all heard the shocking news of successful people committing suicide or overdosing on drugs. Success does not provide all the answers we're searching for. The song "I'm Accepted" by DeGarmo and Key contains these lyrics:

> *I may not be rich*
> *Don't wear fashion clothes*
> *Don't live in a mansion*
> *Don't have much that shows*
> *Never won a contest in popularity*
> *Don't have much to offer*
> *But Jesus loves me*
> *I'm accepted by the One who matters most* [3]

I'm going to discuss four truths I learned many years ago. Acceptance is a thread that runs through each of them. Of course, acceptance isn't the only thread you'll find. I imagine you'll be able to glean other biblical truths that weave themselves into the story. But acceptance is the thread we'll follow.

I'm going to take a layman's view of the Prodigal Son, as taught by Jesus. Jim, our main character introduced in the first chapter, is our prodigal who, like many of us, took numerous steps in search of acceptance.

You might think the prodigal left home in rebellion, that he wasn't really in search of anything but his own selfish desires. I argue only part of that is true. At the root of all rebellion is the desire for acceptance, for love, and for a place to belong. The story of the Prodigal Son is multifaceted and this viewpoint is one of many we can infer from this parable. No matter what the underlying reason, if you look at each step we take away from God, the one word that brings us back into right fellowship with Him is the word "acceptance." God's acceptance is always available when we're ready to return home. We, for our part, just need to accept what God offers.

No matter where you are in your struggle, no matter the circumstances, no matter the questions you ask, or the answers you seek, and no matter with whom you wrestle, I hope you will see God's acceptance of you just as you are. I also hope in the end you'll find, as Jim did, the end of the struggle for acceptance, which in turn completely changed his future. He was no longer dead, but alive.

Chapter Four:

The Parable of the Prodigal Son

According to Nelson's Illustrated Bible Dictionary, a parable is "a short, simple story designed to communicate a spiritual truth, religious principle, or moral lesson." [4] Jesus told many parables, on a variety of different subjects. Some of His parables give everyday examples to help His audience understand or to demonstrate a point. In others, Jesus clouded the meaning and His disciples had to ask for clarification.

In Luke, chapter 15, starting in verse 11, Jesus tells the story of a father with two sons. The younger is commonly known as the Prodigal Son. I've heard a prodigal is characterized by wasteful spending. The younger son clearly fits that definition. However, when I compare the two brothers I can expand that definition.

Although the parable reveals truths about both sons, the story focuses on the younger. As the story unfolds, the younger asks his father for his inheritance early and then leaves for a distant country where he squanders his money on wild living. With all his money gone, he finds himself slowly starving to death. When he realizes his father's servants have better lives in comparison to his current situation, he finally decides to return home. Before we dive into the story too deeply, we should hear how Jesus told the story first.

Luke 15:11-32 states:

> *11 Jesus continued: There was a man who had two sons.*
>
> *12 The younger one said to his father, "Father, give me my share of the estate." So he divided his property between them.*
>
> *13 Not long after that, the younger son got together all he had, set off for a distant country and there squandered his wealth in wild living.*
>
> *14 After he had spent everything, there was a severe famine in that whole country, and he began to be in need.*
>
> *15 So he went and hired himself out to a citizen of that country, who sent him to his fields to feed pigs.*
>
> *16 He longed to fill his stomach with the pods that the pigs were eating, but no one gave him anything.*
>
> *17 When he came to his senses, he said, "How many of my father's hired servants have food to spare, and here I am starving to death!*
>
> *18 I will set out and go back to my father and say to him: Father, I have sinned against heaven and against you.*
>
> *19 I am no longer worthy to be called your son; make me like one of your hired servants."*
>
> *20 So he got up and went to his father. But while he was still a long way off, his father saw him and was*

filled with compassion for him; he ran to his son, threw his arms around him and kissed him.

21 The son said to him, "Father, I have sinned against heaven and against you. I am no longer worthy to be called your son."

22 But the father said to his servants, "Quick! Bring the best robe and put it on him. Put a ring on his finger and sandals on his feet.

23 Bring the fattened calf and kill it. Let's have a feast and celebrate.

24 For this son of mine was dead and is alive again; he was lost and is found." So, they began to celebrate.

25 Meanwhile, the older son was in the field. When he came near the house, he heard music and dancing.

26 So he called one of the servants and asked him what was going on.

27 "Your brother has come," he replied, "and your father has killed the fattened calf because he has him back safe and sound."

28 The older brother became angry and refused to go in. So his father went out and pleaded with him.

29 But he answered his father, "Look! All these years I've been slaving for you and never disobeyed your orders. Yet you never gave me even a young goat so I could celebrate with my friends.

30 But when this son of yours who has squandered your property with prostitutes comes home, you kill the fattened calf for him!"

31 "My son," the father said, "you are always with me, and everything I have is yours.

32 But we had to celebrate and be glad, because this brother of yours was dead and is alive again; he was lost and is found."

I've heard numerous sermons on this portion of Scripture. There are hidden truths in these few passages. In the mid 1980's during one of my Air Force assignments, I was stationed in Oklahoma. My friend, Joe, told me the people of Jesus's day would be very familiar with this parable. Joe was both a Latin and a Hebrew scholar. He stated he was able to trace the story, in various forms, back hundreds of years before it was recorded in Luke's Gospel as well as the parable's various meanings based on how it was told through the generations. He was especially enthusiastic about how Jesus told the parable. Over coffee one afternoon, we discussed what he learned and the meanings of this story. Although I'd heard and read the story many times, Joe opened my mind to different possible interpretations of not only this parable but also many others.

Joe brought this parable to life. He talked about the people in the story as if he knew them. He put himself in their world and was able to make the story unique. Since we've completed reading the parable directly from the Bible, let's use our imaginations and think what it might have been like for Jim.

CHAPTER FIVE:

THE JOURNEY BEGINS

I often wonder about details left out of a biblical story. Scripture identifies a person, but we know little about their life events. What follows is a paraphrased version of the parable we just read. I took some time to consider what the prodigal may have thought or what may have transpired in his life by providing extra details as I see them. If we join the younger son on his journey, what might that look like?

In our version of Jesus's parable, we join the young man as he sits daydreaming on a hillside watching over his father's grazing animals. We eavesdrop on his internal conversation.

I hate this place! Surely, I can't be the only one who hates the place where he grew up. I mean really, really hate it. Maybe I'm strange like my older brother tells me. His words echo in my brain some days. He says, "Jim, you're so strange." And, then chuckles as if he made a joke only he understands.

My older brother is the family favorite. Maybe we're close, but I still hate it when I have to work for him. He always calls me "James" to irritate me, but "Jim" the rest of the time. Oh, how I hate that. My father always calls me James and I hate that too. My mom calls me "Jimmy," as if I'm still her little boy.

Yes, I hate this place. I'm sitting here doing my "job" just as I was told. My brother instructed me to take the sheep over the ridge and let them graze until dusk. What a way to waste a day. After giving me orders, he made the snide comment, "Don't mess up this simple task, okay?" When I didn't respond, his parting words were, "Okay, Jaaames?!" I turned and glared at him. He knew he'd successfully gotten under my skin.

I can't remember when I wasn't dreaming about getting away from here. My family is important in this community and in the surrounding area. No, that's not true. My father is important, I'm not. He's a respected man and our ranch is successful. We have a nice house, plenty of food, and good clothes. Yes, life here is good. It just isn't enough for me. I hate it here!

I was about seven when I realized my fame and fortune wasn't going to be made sitting on a dusty hillside watching a bunch of animals eat. My future is out there somewhere. There's more to this life than my father's ranch. I knew ten years ago when we visited the big city for the first time. The nearby village is as dusty and dry as the ranch and nothing ever happens.

We walk down the sidewalks and everyone greets my father and mother. They say things like, "It's good to see you today." "Oh, how nice to have you in town." What they really want is his business, the opportunity to sit and talk with him, or ask his advice on some boring matter. After he completed his scheduled business, we'd make our way to the village square and he'd take his place among the most respected people. That's the worst. We sit for hours while he imparts his wisdom to all those in attendance. My mother would say, "Your father is so wise, you should listen." Ugh. It's so boring.

When my brother and I were older we were allowed to go off on our own. It's amazing that our family's reputation allows us so much freedom. Merchants didn't dare offend the family and risk my father's future business. With that knowledge I can do almost anything I want, even if it's causing trouble. Of course my brother says, "Stop it, what if father finds out?" He couldn't fool me with his two-faced ways. He likes doing bad things just as much as I do. I was ultimately bored with our village, just as I was with our ranch.

But, I remember our visit to the city like it was yesterday. The sights, the sounds, the crowds, the merchants buying and selling items I never knew existed. The smells of the different foods were carried to my senses from restaurants as exotic as the names emblazoned on the windows and doors. My mother warned me, "Stay close. Catch up, don't get behind." But, I was mesmerized. This is where I wanted to be. I drank it all in until two fingers grasped my ear and pulled me along. My father's painful grip got my attention and his pace, which was far too fast for my little legs, made the city pass in a blur. His stern lecture is long forgotten but the images of the city are burned into my memory.

The next day the entire family accompanied my father as he conducted business. We two boys were supposed to listen and learn. And, learn I did. I learned that here in the big city, my father wasn't as important. He wasn't a big shot. He actually had to tell people his name and they didn't seem impressed. When father's business concluded, we headed home.

The journey home took four long days. My father wanted to make the journey an "adventure", so we camped each night, stopping early so we could explore. Each night, as we lay awake in our own tent, my brother and I discussed the day's events and what we'd discovered. I wanted to talk about the city. My brother didn't. He couldn't believe our family wasn't known and said he'd never leave the village and the comforts the family name provided. "What? That's just crazy," was my reply. I loved that our family name meant nothing in the city. I told him, "I'm going to go back there and make a name for myself. You'll see, the next time the family comes to the city, people will know me."

Every day since that first trip to the city I've dreamed about the day when I'll leave all this behind and live my own life. I've reached the age when it won't be long. I can leave and no one can stop me. How many times did my father tell me, "You are young and there is so much you don't understand. The world is a dangerous place. Slow down and when you're ready you can go." I'd argue, "I want to go now!" "But son, you are not old enough." was always his retort. He'd then begin the usual lecture. "James," he'd say in his most serious tone, "I know this life seems mundane to a young man. But this is good work. This is Godly work. It's work that seems unimportant, but it provides a means for people throughout the country to live." Then he'd look me squarely in the eyes, make a dramatic pause and continue, "You may not understand it now but one day, when you are older, you will. Life will take on a different focus. You will understand what God expects of you. You will seek His favor and want to reach out to help your fellow man."

If he's feeling especially righteous, he brings up the family name. Oh, I'd actually volunteer to tend the flocks on this barren hill to avoid that. I'd look past him sitting in his overstuffed, leather chair and see the far hills. That's where I want to be, not here listening to the lecture I've heard a hundred times. He starts by saying, "A good name is worth more than gold, you know. James, you don't only represent yourself, you represent the family. When people see you, they see me. They see your mother. They see your grandparents. And, like it or not, they draw conclusions from you about all of us." He would conclude, "James, be careful *how you treat your family's name. Respect it and it will serve you well your entire life."*

Once, when I was exasperated with ranch life, I cut the lecture short when I screamed, "When will I be old enough?"

With a heavy sigh, my father's answer was specific, and his words carried a sense of sadness, "When you complete your schooling and turn 18."

I've heard people say, "Time flies when you are having fun," but time has dragged on and on. I never mentioned leaving again. But, his answer burned in my heart and I never forgot it. Next week is graduation. My grades weren't great, but who cares, I'm still graduating. And, to top it off, I'm going to turn 18 a month after graduation. Watch out world here I come!"

As the sun dipped below the hills, Jim's daydreaming came to an end. He got up, brushed the dust off his backside, and began to drive the animals back toward the corrals. Every day for the next week was a repeat of this day. As graduation approached, the more moody and unpleasant Jim became.

When graduation finally arrived, Jim's parents hosted a huge party. "A reason to celebrate," his father said. "You only graduate once," his father shouted to be heard above the crowd gathered in their yard. The summer sun shone warm on Jim's face. The grass was a brilliant green and the trees, with their massive canopies of emerald leaves, provided cool shade. Jim thought how much he disliked standing in the sun. The heat reminded him of work. He stepped under the trees welcoming the 20-degree drop in temperature. His brother bumped him, wrapping his arm around Jim's shoulder. "Nice party, Jim. Although I had my doubts, I'm glad you graduated." Jim tilted his head back and laughed long and hard. "You and me both." His eye sparkled with joy. His brother was genuinely proud of his accomplishment and Jim liked the way it made him feel.

Even as the party moved into high gear, Jim's mind was elsewhere. Many guests were family friends and his father's business associates. Jim made the rounds socializing with a few. During small talk, Jim inquired about business opportunities in the city. Family friends and business associates seemed to be puzzled by his questions. Their general feeling was the city was no place for him. Jim received that unspoken message loud and clear. "Well, we'll see," Jim muttered under his breath.

As the party wore on, Jim's mother came over, wrapped her arms around him, and spoke quietly, "I'm so proud of you son. Jimmy, you're a man now and can take your rightful place beside your father and brother, securing the family's future on the ranch."

Jim was shocked. "*She must be kidding*," he thought. "*My future isn't on the ranch but out there in the distance, where no one knows me or my family. I won't stay one extra minute in this god-forsaken place.*" His mother kissed him on the cheek and her smile conveyed the anticipation that he would do what she expected. Jim decided then and there he'd reject any of his parent's plans for him. Every family may have unspoken expectations, but he wouldn't accept or participate in theirs. His mother looked at him perplexed as she felt him tense in her embrace. She rubbed his back as she hugged him one more time then smiled as she released him. After a brief hesitation, she asked what was wrong. Suddenly, someone called her name. As she greeted a friend from town, she didn't notice as Jim sidestepped into the crowd and walked briskly away. Soon the sun was replaced by cool evening breezes. When no one was looking, Jim left and sat alone for a long time sulking. Finally, after the last guest departed, he went to his room. As he drifted to sleep, Jim again promised himself, "*I will never accept their plans for me.*"

Early the next morning, Jim awoke with a start as his father shouted, "Get up! Get up! A man can't sleep in on a work day." Then his father laughed when the startled new graduate, stumbled out of bed angry at such a rude awakening.

"You'd think I'd be able to sleep in at least a few days after graduation." Jim grumbled. "It's five o' clock in the morning." he yelled. "Don't I get to take a break?"

"No, James" his father chided, laughing at his shocked expression. "You're a man and a man must earn his way in the world, starting today."

There were only 30 days left until that longed-for eighteenth birthday. Days seemed to drag, but his birthday eventually arrived. The party was scheduled to start in a few hours and he had plans to thoroughly enjoy himself. In anticipation of the festivity, Jim returned from the fields earlier than normal, cleaned himself up, and got ready to party.

He couldn't remember a bigger bash ever being held on the ranch and it was for him alone. Jim appreciated that party invitations were relegated to only his friends from town and the nearby farms. "I'm a man and a man can have his own friends at his own party. Leave the family friends out in the cold" he said under his breath. After a brief appearance, the family left Jim and his host of friends to party until dawn if they chose.

Jim laughed and danced with newfound freedom. He couldn't remember when he'd had a better time. But he felt something stirring within him. Slowly at first, but consistently, he felt something beginning to change. Although he didn't understand why, a sense of restlessness built as the night progressed.

Just past 3:00 a.m. friends started to say goodbye and head back to town. With each departure, Jim was more aware of his restlessness. As more and more of his friends headed home, things began to quiet down. For a short time, Jim had been able to forget this was the same dusty, barren piece of land he hated so much. Over the years, he'd been told that every place had the potential to be good or bad, depending on a person's attitude. "Hogwash!" he shouted, "Some places must be better. Any place has to be better." It was the same sentence he said to himself over the years to convince himself he'd be happier away from this dusty farm in the middle of nowhere.

Jim was alone in the silence. The sun hadn't begun to lighten the horizon but, with the new day, the loneliness crept back and brought a sense of anger. It made him feel as if he didn't belong, had never belonged. All he wanted to do was leave. Like a silent scream building to a climax, Jim felt he was about to explode.

The brilliant night sky was breathtaking with stars stretching as far as his eye could see. But, his gaze wasn't captured by the celestial view. All he could see were the ugly, barren hills where in a few short hours, he'd be expected to take the animals to pasture in the hot sun. Remembering the promise, he made thirty days prior, he yelled, "HA! I reject my family's expectations. I'm eighteen. Do you hear me? I'm done. I'm free!" Startled, some of the animals scattered to the far side of the corral. "That's fine, you stupid creatures," he said not realizing they had no idea what he was saying. "I'll never trail after you on the dusty roads, I'll never clean your stalls, or feed you again. I'm free and I don't care about you."

As he turned on his heel and headed back to the house, a new determination grew with each step. It was time to carry out his plans. He initiated the mental checklist he started many years ago. He realized this was the biggest day of his life.

By the time he heard someone in the kitchen, his small bundle was packed. He decided a new wardrobe without any work clothes would fit his new high standards. His biggest issue was the lack of money but, if he played his cards right, he'd soon have plenty of cash.

As the family gathered for breakfast, he could hardly contain his excitement. His mother commented, "Jimmy, you must have enjoyed your party. You can hardly sit still."

"It was great, Mother. Today is going to be a terrific day too. I turned 18 yesterday."

A fond smile crossed her face. A smile that only a mother could produce. "I know. I've been counting."

His brother looked over the rim of his coffee cup and said slyly, "Jim, don't worry about all the excess energy. Little brother, I know how to work it off."

Ignoring his brother's verbal jab, Jim asked, "Father, may I speak to you in your office? I need to discuss something with you personally. It's a thought I've had for awhile and only you're able to address it. I won't keep you long."

His father nodded. "All right but make it quick before the morning gets away from us."

Jim followed his father into the office and watched as he took his usual place in the overstuffed leather chair. Jim was suddenly lost in thought as he remembered this room was the last to warm up since the sun peeked through the window late in the day. He bent slightly and looked out the window where leaves on the tree outside danced in the breeze. As the day grew old, the dance always changed. As a boy, when the days started hot, he recalled he would sit in this room enjoying the coolness and watching the dancing leaves. That little memory drew him back to when he was young and felt a smile grow on his face. He ran his hand along the edge of the old furniture. The wood was worn smooth from use. He reached out and touched the blanket his mother made that now draped over the back of the couch. He remembered how she wrapped it around him on cold mornings.

Abruptly, the memories were banished from his mind by his father's stern voice. "James, stop your daydreaming and tell me what you want."

A flaring anger fueled his determination as he sat on the edge of the couch, "Father, I'll get right to the point. A few years back, I asked you a question. Do you remember?"

"Remember a question you asked me years ago? No, James, I can't say I do."

"I wanted to leave the ranch and head out on my own. Make my fortune. Mark my own destiny. Do you remember now?"

"Oh, yes I do. You mean the one about leaving home and striking out on your own to the big city, right?"

"Yes, father, that's the one. Do you remember what the stipulations were? What did you tell me were my two conditions?"

When his father shook his head, Jim confidently leaned forward and pointed his finger toward his father. "Father, I asked when I could leave. You stated when my schooling was done and I turned eighteen. Well, father, I graduated a month ago and I turned eighteen yesterday. I intend to leave."

"James, this is nonsense. Are you telling me…"

"Yes," Jim interrupted, "that's exactly what I'm telling you. My bags are packed and I'm leaving today."

"James, listen to me. You're a man now. I'm not sure if you understand what that means, but you're going to have to decide what your values are. We raised you with specific values, in Godly wisdom, in faith. You must decide what your faith means to you, and how you're going to live."

Jim leaped off the couch and melodramatically raised his hands above his head, "Father, please, please for the love of God, no more lectures." Standing with one arm outstretched, he pointed directly at his father's face and said, "You're right. I have to decide for myself. Your faith is not my faith. Your values are no longer my values. I reject all of it."

A sad expression slowly crept over his father's face. His father sat motionless as he appeared to age. Those simple words made everything he'd accomplished seem worthless. He suddenly looked old and tired. Jim looked on with little pity. At first, he wasn't sure if the old man even comprehended what he was saying. However, he now saw the truth register on his father's face and realized his plan was going to blossom more beautifully than he dreamed.

"Oh," his father said weakly. "You mean you really are leaving today?" His father's voice, no longer the voice of authority, trembled when he spoke. It was now a voice that registered loss, failure, and pain.

"Yes, I leave as soon as we're finished. I have one last item of business." Jim emphasized the word "business," because that was what his father understood. Comprehending that their roles were now reversed, Jim made his demands.

"I'm joint heir of the family fortune. When you die, I'm entitled to half of what you own. I want my half now. I realize you aren't dead yet, but look at it this way, when you are, you won't owe me anything. When I make my own fortune, I won't need anything from you ever again. Even if you refuse, I'm still leaving."

"Jimmy, please think about what you are doing. Think about what you are saying." The pained expression on the old man's face was telling, but the young man's victory was sealed when his father called him "Jimmy" for the first time.

"No! Father," Jim insisted, "I know what I'm entitled to and I'm asking for it now. Make a decision. I don't have enough money saved because you never paid me enough. So, if I fail, if I starve, it will be your fault, not mine. I'm only asking for what's rightfully mine and what I'll receive anyway when you're dead and gone."

"Okay, okay. I hear you," his father wearily replied. "I never thought you felt this way. I'll get your money although it may take awhile."

Jim was adamant, "No, Father, I want it now. Give me what you have in the safe and I'll take a check for the rest. The day is wasting away and there's work to be done, remember? Let's get going," he continued sarcastically.

With trembling hands, this mountain of a man who'd never faltered before anyone, wrote a check for a very large amount. He then removed an equally large stack of bills from the safe. The overwhelming sense of sadness and betrayal was now etched on the man's face. It wasn't the financial loss that pained the old man so deeply. The personal loss of his son before his very eyes was more then he could bear. Jim grabbed the cash and check and with a half-hearted salute, placing his thumb and forefinger to his forehead, "See ya." was all he said.

With a sense of success, Jim confidently walked into his bedroom and picked up his backpack. He kicked a piece of trash across the room and realized his room was a mess. "What a pig sty. Good riddance!" As he flung open the door, his mother paused in reading her morning Scriptures and gave Jim her full attention. "Jimmy, what's wrong?"

Jim smiled, "Nothing, I'm heading out on my own. Goodbye." She sat frozen in shock; unable to move, speak, or cry at the callous words of her baby boy.

Jim promptly departed, leaving the front door wide open, another first in a day filled with them. No one would ever tell him what to do again.

His first step as a real man led to his second and a third. Soon he was across the yard. With each step, Jim reveled in his sense of freedom and success.

As he left the yard, his brother called out and asked, "Jim, when are you going to start work today?"

As Jim passed his brother, he gave a big smile and a certain hand gesture guaranteed to make his brother wonder, "What in the world is going on?" Tossing his backpack into the backseat, he glanced down at his watch, 7:59 a.m. His plans were right on schedule. As his car accelerated sending dust clouds high in the air, Jim checked the rearview mirror. He couldn't even see the house through the haze.

There was only one stop left, the town bank. The teller's eyes grew wide as she noted the check's large amount. Jim assumed she was jealous. He smiled and stated emphatically, "Yep, it's all mine. Just give me the cash and I'm gone."

Chapter Six:
The Nightmare Starts

Out on the road, Jim's sense of freedom and adventure set him on cloud nine. At the end of the first day, he stopped at the fanciest hotel he could find. He requested the finest suite and ordered a massive meal including the most expensive wine in the house. He was having an adventure, but it wouldn't involve camping. Stretching out on the bed with a sigh of contentment he said, "Man, now this is living."

He got up at 10:00 a.m. and treated himself to a very late breakfast. The waiter gave him a quizzical look when Jim proclaimed, "This tastes so much better at 11:00 a.m. than it does at 5:00 a.m." At the end of the second day, Jim felt confident he was settling in to his new life of luxury. He promised himself, "I'll never go back to my old life because this is what I deserve."

On the third day he picked up a hitchhiker with long hair and worn clothes, but who had a ready smile. They were about the same age. Jim didn't know it, but this chance encounter was about to radically change his life.

"Where are you heading?" Jim asked.

"East, just like you. I'll go as far as you and be happy with that. Once I get into the city, I'll be home."

"I'm just moving there. I'm heading out on my own."

"That's great. Why don't you come home with me? You can crash at my place. It'll give you a place to start."

Jim readily accepted the invitation and recounted stories of his village and family, including his powerful desire to escape. In return, Jim's new friend told tales of amazing foods and activities. Jim was mesmerized. There were tales of parties that lasted for days, women as exotic as their names, and countless other unique opportunities some of which made Jim blush and comment, "I've never heard of such things. I was taught such things are sinful and should be avoided."

With a deep laugh and a clap of his hands, his new friend exclaimed, "All those things you were taught were to keep you from having fun. Stick with me and you'll have times like never before. Besides, if you don't like them you don't have to do them."

Jim was warmly welcomed by his new best friend's family as well as many others, all eager to help him get established. He rented a fabulous apartment and filled it with stylish furniture. The housewarming party lasted three days and at one point Jim exclaimed, "I thought my parents knew how to throw a party, but this one blows my mind."

Before long Jim became well known. He went to the best clubs, the finest restaurants, and the preeminent entertainment events throughout the city. He was always good for a party and friends never hesitated to stop by and stay a few days. Jim was always in the company of good-looking women and everyone thought he was the luckiest man around. If his friends needed a little help, they could count on Jim, as long as they promised to pay him back. It was commonplace for people to stop and greet him on the street. Jim realized that in the city he had become what his father was in *that* small, insignificant village.

All too soon he felt uneasy as his supply of cash began to dwindle. Friends who owed him money disappeared or made excuses for not paying. Girlfriends, who once hung on his arm, were too busy to spend time with him. With his rent due and bill collectors demanding payment, Jim needed to find work, but work he was willing to do was hard to find. One day after turning down a low paying position, Jim returned to his swank apartment only to find an eviction notice tacked to his door. So, Jim did the only thing that came to his mind. He sold his furniture and high-end collectables at a fraction of what they cost and paid his rent for another month. Thirty days later and after another grand party, he found himself on the street. With nowhere else to go, Jim ended up on his best friend's couch. After only three days, his buddy woke Jim with the tip of his shoe. He snarled, "Dude, how long you gonna stay on my couch?"

"I'm not sure. I can't find work. You know things are tough right now," was Jim's meek response.

"Well," Jim's so-called friend snapped, "You can't stay here anymore unless you can pay something for the use of the couch. Do you have a couple hundred dollars for the week?"

Jim's mounting anger was unmistakable in his voice. "Are you serious? After all I've done for you? This is what our friendship means, a miserable two hundred bucks?"

His false friend simply looked at him and said, "I don't owe you anything. Grab you stuff. Get out and don't come back."

How could all his friends disappear? People who once greeted him with a hug now pushed him aside. Those who owed him money scoffed at his requests for repayment. The restaurant owner who welcomed him night after night slammed the door and suggested he find something to eat in the dumpster. No one would give him the time of day, never mind a job, a handout, or a free meal.

Time became a blur as each day dragged into the next. He wandered the streets begging, but never received enough food or coins. He seemed to be hungry all the time and soon became accustomed to digging through dumpsters. Most days he sat on a street corner until someone gave him enough money to eat.

Jim was sitting on a block of stone at the corner of two streets one particularly sad day, hoping for but not receiving a little mercy. He held a simple cardboard sign that read, "Homeless. Anything helps. God bless." It had been two days since the last time food filled his belly. Suddenly, Jim noticed an old man on the opposite corner intently staring at him. To his surprise, the old man called him by name. "James? You are James aren't you? I know your father," he said. "He's a very Godly man and good business man too. I respect him. Listen, there's a man outside of town who will hire you. Go see him if you want a job." He placed a folded piece of paper in Jim's hand.

"Thank you," Jim mumbled. With that, the old man turned and walked away. Jim never saw him again.

Jim unfolded the paper to find an address with directions as well as a twenty-dollar bill. It wasn't much but now he could finally eat. "The old man knows my father?" he thought out loud. "You'd think he'd give me more than a lousy twenty bucks and a job offer. Huh, guess he really does know him. They're both tight-fisted old men." With a laugh, Jim headed to a place where food was cheap and so was the beer.

Several more nights passed before he decided to check on this so-called job. Jim was forced to walk since his car had been repossessed weeks ago. The address led him to a run-down pig farm. When he asked if they were hiring, a woman at the main house directed him to the foreman who was standing in a nearby field. The foreman spoke with such authority Jim knew the man didn't play well with others. Realizing he'd turned down better positions in the city, he secretly hoped there was no work here.

"I was told a bum named James would come looking for work," the foreman snarled. "I heard you have some skill with animals."

Jim puffed up his chest, "Yup, that's right, I have skills. I go by Jim."

He rapidly deflated, however, when the foreman said, "Sure you do. James, you'll start slopping hogs in the morning." To Jim's surprise and horror, he was offered a job. His rumbling stomach helped him decide to accept the offer. He was told to sleep in the barn, the single meal was in the evening, and work started at the familiar 5:00 a.m.

His first arduous day lasted well past nightfall. When he was finally finished, all he could think about was dinner. He was way past hungry and grabbed a plate and got in line. The food hit the plate with a dismal *plop!* Along with a stale slice of bread, he ravenously ate what little he was given and thought, "I can't even call this food. The slop I fed the pigs looked better than this."

One weary day followed another. The harsh sun grew more oppressive as the days wore on. With no food and no water, the repressive heat took its toll. One scorching day Jim felt light-headed and sat down in the shade. In the distance, he saw the foreman stomping toward him. With hands on his hips, the foreman thundered, "James, did someone say for you to take a break?"

"No, but I feel faint. I just need to take a small break," was Jim's weak reply.

"Get back to work or you'll be feeling more than faint." the foreman barked.

Jim wiped a hand over his sweating face. "It's so hot. Could I have some water? It's one hundred degrees in the shade."

A sly smile etched itself on the foreman's unforgiving face. "If it's too hot in the shade, you don't have to stand in the shade." A swift kick sent Jim rolling into the merciless sun and back to slopping the hogs.

Sunset finally granted some relief from the heat and long after the sun disappeared, Jim made it back to the food line. The foreman greeted him with the cynical comment, "If you want to eat our food, you need to work faster and not take breaks in the shade. Do you understand, Jaaaames?"

Clutching his empty dinner plate, a perplexed Jim inquired, "I don't understand what this has to do with my dinner?"

The foreman's hands were a blur as he snatched the plate. Bending at the waist, his face mere inches from Jim's face, the foreman snarled, "You'll get no dinner tonight because you were caught loafing. Is that clear?"

"Yes, sir." Jim weakly replied. As the young man turned to walk away, the foreman planted his foot squarely in the middle of his back and shoved. The unexpected assault sent Jim sprawling into the dirt while the other workers howled with laughter.

Missing dinner became a nightly ritual. If Jim was early, he was sent back to the fields. When he returned, it was too late to eat. If it took too long to complete work for the day, he went hungry. The foreman appeared to get a sick pleasure out of denying the workers, especially Jim, food. In desperation, Jim found he could pick through the pig slop and find enough to take away some of the hunger pains. The slop wasn't bad if you disregarded the taste and smell. It wasn't long before Jim skipped the miserable dinner ritual altogether.

Payday forced Jim's participation in yet another ritual. The farm owner himself handed out pay in cash for the past week. When it was his turn, Jim watched as his portion was counted. Twice Jim pointed out that his pay seemed to be short by a substantial amount.

"Listen," the owner said sharply, "I agree to pay you a wage. You work and I pay. It's that easy. I deduct the cost of meals and lodging from your pay. That leaves the amount I gave you. Do you understand?"

"Yes, sir," Jim replied, then stepped aside for the next man to step up for his wages.

However, the payday ritual wasn't quite over. The foreman stepped in front of Jim and demanded, "I need my fee." Suddenly Jim understood. As he waited in line for his pay, Jim noticed each person ahead of him, made his way to the foreman. The two men would talk briefly, the foreman often placing a hand on the worker's shoulder before they separated.

Jim asked, "How much?"

"James, I normally take half, but today, you get the special. Three-quarters," came the retort. "Next time don't make me come looking for you."

Feeling totally defeated, Jim handed over three-quarters of his wages and returned to the disgusting chores that awaited him, the heat that baked his brain, and the miserable existence of his life.

Bleak weeks became months and months became a year. Daily life was an oppressive burden. As Jim lay awake each night he tearfully thought of home. As he laid on his back tears filled his eyes. He realized he missed home and the green grass beneath his feet. He dreamed of afternoon naps under in the cool emerald shade when it was too hot to work. His mouth watered remembering delicious meals. He dreamed of cool water splashing over him, washing the dust and grim off after a hard day in the field and of how clean clothes felt against clean skin. He remembered the harsh words he'd spoken to his father, how he didn't really say goodbye to his mother, and the disrespect he displayed to his brother. The sadness was overwhelming and he slept fitfully until awakened for another day in the seemingly endless cycle. Until one day, as he dipped into the pig slop for a morsel of corn and a slice of rancid mystery meat, he finally realized that if he stayed here much longer he would surely die.

"Why can't I go home?" he pondered.

That first honest question opened a floodgate of thoughts. And the thoughts came faster and faster. There was no stopping them.

> *"My father has many servants who are treated far better than this. I would rather be a servant in my father's house than live another day on this god-forsaken piece of ground. Father's ranch is an oasis compared to this barren land. I miss our little village and how friends greeted us with genuine happiness. What if father refuses to take me back? What if he turned me away? He's a Godly man. He would at least feed me and let me rest awhile. He never turned away hungry strangers. I willingly admit I've disgraced the family name and don't deserve to be called his son. I admit I'd be honored to be considered one of his servants. I could at least know if my mother*

is well and know how my brother is doing. Even if
they turn their backs on me, it will be better than this.
I can't live here another day."

He forgot about work and the heat as he paced, his heart hammering in his chest. For each tormented "what if" he fought back with a positive option. The internal one-way conversation repeated itself all day and into the evening. Then Jim made up his mind. He would leave. The first rays of dawn hadn't brightened the eastern horizon when he packed his few ragged belongings. Before the workday began, Jim turned toward home.

CHAPTER SEVEN:

THE WAY HOME

I f it hadn't been for the kindness of strangers, Jim would have never made it. At one point, he was given a meal and extra food to carry on his journey. One day, overcome by heat, a stranger provided cool water and a place to rest in the shade. On a stormy night, an invitation to sleep in a barn came with a hot meal. Jim knew he smelled and the clothes that hung on his malnourished frame were nothing more than wisps of fabric. Daily he experienced mercy from strangers even though he looked no better than the worse vagabond and certainly didn't deserve any of their generosity.

The normal three-day journey took weeks but, as the area became more familiar, Jim decided to skirt the village. By going around his hometown, he hoped to avoid any dishonor his appearance might bring upon his family.

On the last day, he cried as his foot took the first step onto his father's land. He was finally home. All morning he rehearsed his speech, refining how he would present himself to his father and apologize. He would kneel, lower his head, and say just above a whisper, "Father, I have sinned against Heaven and you. I am not worthy to be called your son. If you would allow it, I would like to be one of your servants. I will serve the family for the rest of my life and will never expect more. I will be loyal to you and will be your most grateful and hardest worker. However, if you say 'no,' I will understand. I apologize for the wrong I have done and the pain I have caused." With each new rendition, he changed a word or a phrase, but what he said never seemed to convey how he felt.

As he rounded a small knoll, the outline of the house finally appeared. Nervously he stopped and took a deep breath, determined with each step to see this through. He exhaled. He inhaled deeply. He straightened his stance and took another step. Suddenly, Jim saw movement at the top of the hill; someone was running toward him shouting. The words were indistinct, muffled by distance. Shielding his eyes from the sun to get a better view, he realized it was father. Jim had never seen his father run anywhere. Jim mouthed a silent cry as tears streaked his dirt-caked face. "*What have I done?*" Jim thought. "*The pain I caused is beyond description.*"

As his father slid to a stop, Jim collapsed to his knees, bowed his head, and sobbed "Father I have sinned against Heaven and against…"

Instead of recriminations, his father grabbed him by the shoulders and lifted him to his feet. Despite his appearance and the pungent order, Jim was wrapped in a firm hug and a welcome kiss. "James! James! You're alive. You're alive!" his father cried repeatedly.

As the fierce hug ended, Jim once again began his speech. "Father, I have sinned against Heaven and against you. I'm no longer worthy to be called your son…"

Ignoring Jim's pleas, his father seized him again and hauled him up the hill onto the front porch where he ripped the rags off his son's body, ordering a servant to bring new clothes. Then, as a symbol of belonging, his father slipped the family ring on his finger. Lastly, a servant brought new sandals and placed them on his feet.

All Jim's arguments died in his throat. He couldn't utter a word. His mind couldn't comprehend what happened. He couldn't grasp this kind of welcome. "*I don't deserve this,*" he thought. "*It's like the greatest dream I've ever had. Will I awake only to realize it was only a dream?*"

He tried to shake off the bewilderment of this experience, but doubts gave way to this one simple truth, his father loved and accepted him just as he was. He thought his father would be beside himself with rage, but instead showed amazing love and compassion.

More tears welled up in his eyes as he spotted his mother standing in the doorway. She was clearly weeping. Her hands covered her mouth momentarily before she brushed away her own tears. The one thing he couldn't deny was her smile. Despite the tears that now flowed freely, not caring if anyone noticed, her smile was radiant and conveyed all he needed to know. He knew he was home and was loved.

His mother approached and reached out to embrace him. Her embrace was long and strong. As she released her son, she stepped back. She paused, stared into his eyes. One hand still grasped his forearm. The other hand reached up to his face, lightly touching his cheek. Her only words were "Jimmy, I've missed you."

"Mother, I'm so sorry for all…" Jim started but lost his voice as the emotions overwhelmed him, the remaining words never escaped his mouth. As only a mother can, without a spoken word, Jim knew all was well between them.

The tender moment was broken at the sound of his father's booming voice. "Tonight we celebrate. Prepare a feast! My son, who was dead, is now alive. Come everyone, tonight we celebrate!"

CHAPTER EIGHT:

A LITTLE BACKSTORY

I enjoy augmenting an existing story to bring characters to life. My paraphrased version is my endeavor to do just that. Paraphrasing is taking a story and rewriting or changing it to achieve clarity or highlight a special meaning. When I look at a story, I ask questions and attempt to discover answers by retelling the story. What was life like for the prodigal son? How difficult would it have been on a day-to-day basis?

Clearly, the prodigal son had a few attitude problems and disliked living on the family farm. It's typical for a young adult to feel this way. Also, because I focused on the prodigal, I didn't significantly develop the character of the father, mother, or older brother. We have to remember each of those characters has their own personality. I did attempt to show how those personalities impacted the prodigal.

I named the prodigal James because it's an easy name to split into nicknames. As each family member played a role in Jim's life, I wanted to show those distinct differences. Of course, I'm only speculating. When Jesus tells the story, He leaves out the events that led Jim to the point where he wanted to leave home. Before we go much further, let's look at the characters in our story.

The father always called his son "James." This formality reflects the father's authority over his son. It's possible Jim resented that authority. The father ran a successful farming operation and even in hard times his family had enough. In all matters, the father maintained his authority. I believe, the father didn't mean to make his son angry. Jim resented the authority and developed a viewpoint that missed his father's love and concern for his son's welfare. The father only intended good for his son. In spite of his father's intent, the result became a barrier for his son. In the end, the father-son relationship lacked the intimacy the son desired as well as the closeness the father wanted. It's possible that no matter how the father behaved toward his son, the results would have been the same. Often parents find it easier to relate to their younger children than to teenagers. A father makes a funny face and a young child laughs. When older, the same child rolls his eyes and mumbles, "That's stupid." A distance develops between the two generations and the relationship suffers. In this story, it appears the father and son can't relate, but their reunion shows the depth of the father's love. The love was always there, but Jim couldn't see it.

Although the parable doesn't mention a mother, I wanted to include her as a caring, nurturing figure. Sadly, Jim feels she won't let him grow up. I show this by symbolically using the name "Jimmy." As a child grows into adulthood, I think mothers often struggle with the approaching empty nest. When Jim left home, his failure to give her a proper goodbye hug is a pain that will never be forgotten by either mother or child. Parents often experience the pain of the young adult's rebellion. It's often overlooked because the importance of the relationship outweighs the pain. Every parent has a difficult task in raising a child but overlooks the hardship and heartache. When a child matures emotionally they often realize the many sacrifices made on their behalf and the emotional pain they themselves inflicted. It's then, that reconciliation in a strained relationship becomes possible. In our story, Jim's interactions with his mother reflect how he took advantage of his parent's feelings and how a simple act of anger and rebellion created years of regret. All conflict vanished when he returned and became the man his parents hoped he would become. As many parents can attest, years of heartache can be washed away in an instant.

Jim's overbearing brother doesn't hesitate to hold the power of seniority over him. I'm sure through the years the sibling rivalry spilled over into serious confrontations. Anyone who has brothers or sisters knows how to get under a sibling's skin and irritate them to the point of exasperation. This is true in my own life. However, if you asked my two brothers and four sisters, I'm sure they'd invent numerous stories of how I, the fourth child but the eldest brother, annoyed them without mercy. Mind you, all their tales are probably inaccurate and exaggerated. In our story, Jim takes great offense at his brother's authority over him. Although there were moments that reflect their closeness and love for one another over the years, Jim feels justified by holding a grudge against his older brother. Most siblings grow out of these childhood conflicts and have lasting friendships.

Family dynamics are difficult to unravel and often carry life-long scabs we feel the need to pick at. This frequently happens at family gatherings during the Thanksgiving and Christmas seasons. This time to come together and enjoy each other often raises past hurts. Soon an argument is brewing with the potential to ruin the entire celebration. In Luke 15: 32, the arrival of the older brother from the fields has the potential of one such event.

I purposely ended my version of the story before verse thirty-two and intentionally left out the brother's reaction to the prodigal's return. I'm not ignoring this aspect of the story, as it's something we all need to be aware of and deal with in our lives. However, as I mentioned earlier, my focus is on Jim and not his interactions with his brother. This book isn't about the family dysfunction we all have nor how we wrestle with issues of reconciliation and forgiveness within families. Even though that's not my focus, if the Holy Spirit brings it to your attention, you would do well to listen, pray, seek Godly counsel, and work through your family's issues. As we'll discover, reconciliation, forgiveness, and a right relationship with God, as well as our parents and siblings, is possible.

It's important to point out that the older brother is also a prodigal. As I mentioned previously, a prodigal is characterized by wasteful spending. Even though the elder brother never recklessly squandered money or abused the fiscal trust of his father, he is a prodigal. If you've never run away from home or wasted your inheritance on wild living, it doesn't mean you're not a prodigal. The older son never ventured far from the ranch. As a matter of fact, he stated he'd been "slaving" for his father for years. But it isn't always what you do or don't do that reveals the true condition of your heart. Although we don't have much information about the elder son, I'd like to take a moment and examine why he was also a prodigal. We're able to catch a glimpse of his true condition when Jim returns home.

Jim's brother decided not to celebrate his safe return and his father came to talk to him when he refused to come to the party.

His father pleaded with his oldest son to celebrate his brother's safe return but what he received was an earful on all that was wrong. The older son compared his working conditions as equivalent to being a slave. He further pointed out his own righteousness when he admitted he'd "never disobeyed" his father's orders. Of course, he was able to clear the air when he pointed out he'd also been wronged by his father. He pointed out that his father never gave him "even a young goat" to celebrate with his friends. But he didn't stop at telling his father how hard he worked, explaining how deep his loyalty went, or how he endured being victimized. He reminded his father how horrible his other son had been by stating, "...this son of yours who has squandered your property with prostitutes..." (Luke 15:30). Jim's brother is a prodigal trapped in legalism and tradition. All those years he served his father but never grasped all that was at his disposal.

For years, he learned from his father and developed his business skills for only one purpose; to be the next generation to manage the ranch. He could have thrown a hundred parties for his friends, instead he choose to play the victim. His hard work established him as a leader in his community, yet he saw himself as a slave to his father. His father freely gave him everything he owned. He saw all his hard work as a negative. While rich beyond his expectations, he saw himself as a pauper. He was indeed far from his father's ultimate desire for his life.

If I consider both brothers as prodigals, is it possible there are different types of prodigals? I believe the answer is "yes." In the following pages, I use the term "prodigal" differently from the usual interpretation. Even if we use the monetary wastefulness as part of our definition, in a spiritual sense we have all foolishly squandered parts of our lives. For our discussion, I define a prodigal as anyone who is away from God. At some point we are all separated from God. From a layman's perspective I developed three types of prodigals we find around us.

First is the "accidental" prodigal. This prodigal, at what appears as no fault of his own, has never been exposed to church. Possibly this person wasn't raised in a family that attended church on a regular basis so their exposure to religion is severely limited. They may have a belief system from another faith or a combination of different belief systems, but they've never entered into a relationship with Jesus Christ.

Over the years, I've met many people who've never attended church or attended only on an occasional basis, never read the Bible, or understood the spiritual concept of prayer. To these prodigals, churches are relegated to weddings, funerals, or other special occasions. Often, they identify as "Christian" because that's what they've been told. In the past some relative identified this as their faith and they, in turn, accept it without questioning what the label actually means. I began this prodigal's description by stating it appears they are apparently in this category through no fault of their own. It may appear they're not at fault, but let me be clear, these prodigals are 100% responsible for their placement in this category. They often consider Christianity as merely a denomination. They miss the message of the Cross, and they remain spiritually lost.

I once met a young man whose family immigrated to the United States from Czechoslovakia (now known as the Czech Republic) when it was still behind the Iron Curtain. Although the Czech Republic now enjoys many of the same freedoms as other European countries, before the Iron Curtain fell in the 1990's, its citizens had very limited freedom. Saying they immigrated is technically correct, but that term deceptively hides the family's real experiences and accomplishments. His family fled the oppression of the communist government and after years of moving and filing applications, finally received permission to settle in the United States. He told me stories of oppression, of hunger and want, and of how his family ultimately escaped to freedom. Although he was born in United States, it was clear the family history had been passed down. He also stated he was from a Christian family. His next question reveled he was an accidental prodigal. "Isn't church for the weak?" he asked. He identified as a Christian but, in truth, was not. Although aware of the faith within his family history, he was a prodigal. He didn't know what being a Christian meant and admitted he didn't have a personal relationship with Christ or even comprehend what that relationship might entail.

Today, more and more individuals have no exposure to faith, let alone an understanding of the Gospel. As church becomes less important to the typical family, many don't know anyone in their family circle who are religious, exercise their faith in any significant manner, or express a living faith in their daily lives. I've met many people who were in their twenties or thirties and have never attended a church service.

When I was deployed to the Middle East, a young Army soldier attended one of our chapel services because he had nothing else to do. Each Sunday morning, he woke up to the sound of music coming from our chapel tent. On a whim, he decided to check it out. He was in his twenties and had never been to church, never had a Bible, or even thought much about God, faith, or religion. After the service he asked question after question about not only the church but also God, Jesus, and other spiritual matters. His questions ultimately led him to the place where he asked Christ into his life. But, up to that point, he had no concept of his true spiritual condition. He was an accidental prodigal.

The second prodigal, I'll call the "prodigal by choice".

This prodigal knows and attends all the church activities. Our churches are full of fathers, mothers, sons, and daughters who are prodigals, but, like Jim's older brother, have never ventured very far from home. They attend church each week, but in their heart they are just as much a prodigal as Jim was when he left home. They're fluent in religious speech and well-versed in traditions. However, it's all head-knowledge and lacks the heart-knowledge of personally knowing the Savior.

The father, who attends church each week but has a heart that's far away from God, is a prodigal. Who knows why a man would attend church when he doesn't have a personal relationship with Jesus. Maybe he wants to keep peace with his wife or wants to be a good example to his children. Perhaps it's just a habit. Without Christ, attending church every time the doors are open doesn't change your actual condition. You're still a prodigal. Being religious isn't the same as knowing Jesus as Lord. If you're religious without Jesus, you're still spiritually dead but you do so with a religious flair and fit into this second category of prodigals.

What of the mother who attends services regularly but doesn't have a relationship with God? She may attend each week, even by herself, but lacks the heavenly connection on a personal level. She is a prodigal. Does she attend out of a commitment to how she was raised? Does she attend because of the social connections with other church members? Whatever the reason, without a personal relationship with the Creator of the Universe you are lost in your sins and yes, you're still a prodigal.

Children are often less complicated. They attend because they're told they must. Without a personal link to the Cross, many stop attending church as soon as they're able to win the argument with their parents, go off to college, or move to their own home. No matter how you're raised or how much your parents loved the

Lord, unless you have a personal link to the Savior, you're alone. No matter how many online friends you have, you are a prodigal.

Jimmy was one of my best friends. Although he's not related to the Jim in my parable, when we first met, he was a prodigal. When I was seventeen, he was my boss at a local gas station, a job that brings back fond memories. Jimmy was raised in church and his family was heavily invested in their local congregation. However, when Jimmy made a personal connection with the living Savior, his life radically changed. Church was no longer just something to do on a Sunday morning. He had fallen in love with Jesus Christ. And, since he was spiritually changed, his entire life was as well, and that change was easy to see. When Jimmy finally "heard" the Gospel and understood its meaning, he moved from death to life. His family on the other hand, couldn't grasp what had happened to him. They sat week after week, year after year listening to the minister, but couldn't hear the Spirit calling. Although his family was exposed to church and the Gospel, they were all prodigals.

The last prodigal is one we'll call the "soon-to-be-prodigal". These prodigals are firm in their belief and their confession of faith. They may or may not have been raised in church. They may or may not have been exposed to religious teaching. But, a moment came when they decided to follow Jesus. Many can point to a specific place and time when they became a Believer. They served the Lord for years, giving of their time, talents, and resources to support the church, missionaries, and other good works. But over time, their commitment began to fade. The bond they felt to their faith began to fray. This prodigal has no plans to leave his Christian walk. For example, a young man believes his faith is important to him but somewhere along the narrow path he takes an exit and finds himself on a different road. A young woman, who never sees herself outside of faith, takes a different path and one day looks back and wonders how she got to this location. Maybe it was a small compromise at first, a hurt feeling allowed to fester, or a belief contrary to Scripture takes hold, but the exit places this believer on a secondary road. Maybe it's a chance encounter such as Jim had with the hitchhiker in our story. Some chance encounters can completely change our future because they slowly lead us away, down a different path.

This prodigal travels a little further down the secondary road, soon takes another exit, and numerous exits after that. Each exit takes him further from where he started. By the time he realizes how far he's ventured, he feels there's no way to turn back. He never expected to have difficulty finding the way home.

A young woman walks a familiar path but becomes sidetracked for what she believes will be a brief season. As life often does, her life then takes a few twists and turns. Years later she looks back and finds it hard to comprehend how far she's traveled. One thought leads to another and that thought leads to another. Successive thoughts turn into actions. Those actions become habits and, one day, she realizes she's far away with no idea how she got there.

There are many reasons for the slow slide. Both the weariness and the goodness of life can take a toll and the ember that once brought fire to a heart begins to dim. Maybe we search for answers to difficult questions and, not finding a clear answer, begin to doubt. Another possibility is that someone, held in high esteem morally fails us. The list of reasons causing this prodigal to stray is endless, but how it begins is immaterial, the end result is the same. We wander away from faith and soon find ourselves apart from God. Only occasionally do we stop and consider how God became a stranger.

During my high school years, I knew many other teenagers who were Christians. They would profess a strong faith and had plans to serve God their entire lives. However, some of those believers would say, "I just want to have a little fun." They wanted to try a little bit of the wild side of life. They just wanted to take a "break". The sad truth is some prodigals don't come home. I've known many who've died away from God and others who aren't able to make it back. They often share tales of sadness and regret.

The point is prodigals are not only found hanging around a "pig sty". They're all around us. They warm our church pews each week, or work side-by-side with us each day at the office or the factory. Some have never heard the Gospel or about the redemptive power of the Cross. Some join other believers in worship. They sit there week after week, month after month, year after year but consistently miss redemption. Some quote the Bible by chapter and verse. Others wander away for a variety of reasons and a previously cherished relationship fades away. Over the years, I've met many prodigals from each of these categories.

By my personal testimony, I admit I was in the second category of prodigals. I may not have been raised in church, but I often attended. Religious education was a regular part of my childhood schedule. Since my family moved every few years, we often attended a church close to our house. We may check all the usual boxes for what was considered to be Christian, but we weren't an active family of faith.

My uncle was a Baptist minister in Ohio and I heard the Gospel when we visited his church, but I never responded to accept Jesus as my Savior. My uncle gave me a book about John's Gospel and a Bible, but I never read them. Over the years while attending different churches, I'm sure I heard the Gospel message, but in truth I was as lost as if I'd never heard it. During one summer visit, my uncle and his family introduced us to a new church, where for the first time, I actually began thinking about the concept of following Christ.

Each Monday evening that church's pastor visited my family, conducting a short Bible study. Following one of these Bible studies, my life changed. On the third Monday in the month of August, I sat on my couch, asked Jesus Christ to be my Savior and became a born-again Christian. I was only fifteen years old, but that single event set me on a course that has impacted the rest of my life.

I spent over 30 years in the United States Air Force. I traveled to many parts of the United States and also had a fair amount of travel outside the country. I lived in Europe for nearly ten years and had four government paid trips, commonly called deployments, to the Middle East. At every assignment, in every country and in every state, I met people who were prodigals.

My first assignment was at Lackland Air Force Base in Texas. Located outside of San Antonio, Lackland is where all new Air Force recruits go for basic military training. Even after nearly forty years, I still remember stepping off the bus and being "warmly" welcomed by the drill instructors. No matter how many years have passed, anyone who served in a branch of the military never forgets that event. Whether you called them drill sergeants, drill instructors, or military training instructors, the "fond" memories are the same. In that environment it doesn't take long for fellow recruits to open up and share different aspects of their lives.

One young man joined the military to get away from home. Another didn't know what to do with his life, so he said "I do" to Uncle Sam. Another couldn't find work to provide for his family. As is normally the case in basic training, I quickly made new friends from all over the country. They came from big cities and from the countryside. All walks of life were represented. We even had a recruit from the Philippines. As I read my Bible daily and prayed over meals, it didn't take a rocket scientist to grasp that I was a person of faith.

During basic training and the technical school that followed, I began to meet prodigals. Some would readily admit that they were raised in church. Some asked many questions about God, having never been exposed to Christianity. A few prayed, inviting Jesus into their lives, moving from death to life in the highly regulated environment of military training.

From beautiful Lackland Air Force Base to Royal Air Force (RAF) Lakenheath in the United Kingdom, to Plattsburgh, New York, to a little outpost in the mountains of Turkey overlooking Iraq, prodigals were there. There were those who had no interest in God, those who normally attended church services but couldn't tell you why, and men and women who would readily admit, "I was raised in church, but somehow lost my way." With sadness, the last group, would often state, "But that was a long time ago and I'm so far away now." I invited them to church, but they would give an excuse such as, "No, I'm too far gone" or "I'm married now. My spouse wouldn't approve" or "I don't have the right clothes to wear." Excuses are just poor reasons why you don't want to do something and prodigals tend to have many of them.

Of course, there were some who didn't have an excuse. There were those prodigals who accepted the invitation. They soon found out that God was about to intervene in their lives. The acceptance of the simple invitation had the potential to change their lives forever. My 30 years in the Air Force is filled with memories of prodigals who came home, even if they were half-way around the world. Not to the homes where they grew up or the cities or towns they were from, but to God.

After basic training and technical school at Lackland AFB,

my second duty station in the early 1980's was RAF Lakenheath. I still cherish many of the friendships forged during those years. One particular friend was an Airman who worked in the armory. Scott lived directly below me on the second floor of our barracks. Along with Troy and Darren, he became a Believer while in the area of East Anglia, England. All three were baptized by our English pastor on a brisk autumn day in a local river. The four of us became great friends and all shared a bond of faith. However, as is always the case in the military, permanent change of station (PCS) orders will always arrive for someone. Those orders for Troy, Darren, and Scott arrived a year before mine. The pastor of our small fellowship and I drove them to RAF Mildenhall for their flight home. This was long before the dawn of Facebook and I never expected I would see them again.

Flash forward a dozen years. My family was stationed at Minot Air Force Base in North Dakota. Soon after arriving, I left my family and deployed to Cuba. I rejoined my family just before Christmas after a three-month separation. In a rush to buy gifts before the holiday, I was in the local Wal-Mart. While shopping with a sense of urgency, as men often display just before Christmas, I heard a voice calling, "Excuse me sir. Sir! Excuse me."

Turning, I was surprised to see Scott. He said he thought his eyes had played tricks on him. Scott was no longer in the Air Force and was an assistant manager for Wal-Mart. Halfway around the world in a small town in the northern United States and a dozen years between meetings, I bumped into a great friend and brother in the Lord. It was fantastic to be able to worship with him again after so many years. It wasn't long before Wal-Mart transferred Scott to a new store in another state, but the connection we share will last forever.

As chapters unfold, I'll recount a few stories of those prodigals, many of whom found acceptance and answers to many questions they were asking. I'll relate personal stories of people I've met along my journey, who, after accepting a simple invitation, decided to make their way home. These are stories of people who moved from death to life, just as did our friend Jim encountered in the first chapter.

I hope the truths I'll share are not aimed just toward prodigals. The timeless message of the Cross is for all of us. No matter how many years we've walked with the Lord, there is more work to be done in our hearts. In the following pages, I'll share four spiritual truths I learned many years ago. Using the parable of the Prodigal Son, with Jim as our example, and the personal stories of other prodigals we'll meet, let's examine and apply four things that God does not know.

Chapter Nine:
A Wretch Finds Grace

Amazing Grace is a hymn with great significance to many Christians and non-Christians alike. It's my understanding this age-old classic was written by an ex-slaver. John Newton wrote the famous hymn as a personal testimony of his conversion to Christianity. If you read about Newton, you'll find he was raised by a Christian mother who died when he was young. He also admitted he was quick to follow sin but, by his own account, he also enticed others to join him. Newton was a prodigal. His days as mate and ultimately captain on a slave ship impacted Newton to the end of his life. After leaving the slave trade, Newton became a minister who wrote hundreds of hymns. One of his creations was *Amazing Grace,* possibly the most well-known hymn of all. Conceivably born from regret for his past, Newton questioned if he was even redeemable. One of the greatest evils in history, is the practice of buying and selling human beings. It saddens me to know that human trafficking still exists.

Years ago, my military travels took me to Enid, Oklahoma

where I attended a non-denominational, evangelical church which left a lifelong impression on me. The service started with John Newton's famous hymn.

The song leader approached the podium and said, "Please join me in singing *Amazing Grace*." And, they proceeded to sing, "Amazing grace, how sweet the sound that saved someone like me…" I stopped singing in the middle of the first verse. That was a new version I'd never heard, and it completely threw me. For the remainder of the service I contemplated what had happened to one simple word in the first hymn of the morning. That word is "wretch". In my experience the actual words are "Amazing Grace how sweet the sound that saved a wretch like me. I once was lost but now I'm found, was blind but now I see." [5] Substituting the word "someone" for "wretch" may not seem like a significant change to some, but it was important to me and still is. I distinctly remember one other part of the service, when I was greeted by the pastor and inquired about the change of this age-old hymn. As I approached, the pastor stretched out his hand. I took it in a firm handshake and after he welcomed me, I asked. "Pastor, when did they change the words to *Amazing Grace*?"

"Excuse me?" he replied. "Changed the words?"

"Yes sir. 'Amazing Grace, how sweet the sound that saved someone like me…' What happened to the word 'wretch'?"

With a smile, the pastor replied, "Oh, I see. Please understand, I feel 'wretch' is such a harsh word. I, for one, do not consider myself a wretch. I don't think I ever was one."

I looked into the pastor's eyes and even though he was smiling, I said, "Oh no. Pastor, I was a wretch and I needed a Savior." Jim, in my little paraphrased story, was also a wretch. He was also in need of a Savior.

Did Newton select the right word for his famous hymn, or was the pastor correct when he changed that "harsh word"? If a person is described as a wretch, he is a miserable or unhappy person, a person in deep distress or misfortune; someone who is despised. Our English language has multiple adjectives to describe a person in a wretched state: grieving, brokenhearted, and anguished just to name a few. When we're separated from God and realize one day we must give an account of our lives, I would say Newton selected the appropriate word.

I hear people talk about how far the human race has come over the centuries. But have we really come all that far? Has the human condition really improved that much? Jesus recounted this parable more than 2,000 years ago. As I mentioned earlier, my friend Joe informed me that the basic story of the Prodigal Son was centuries old and Jesus was retelling it. It was a story that many, if not all, in Jesus's audience would have been familiar with. Although the age of the story isn't important to our discussion, it shows the human condition hasn't significantly changed. Even if the story is only 2,000 years old, it shows we humans are still struggling with some of the same issues. If the parable is indeed much older, it makes the point even more clear. Every generation, dating back thousands of years, has faced similar struggles.

How many times have parents stated, "My house, my rules?" Young people can't wait to escape all the rules in their parents' house. They want to blaze their own trail and live their own life. Unfortunately in many cases, the results are similar to Jim's. Although it might not be pig slop, I've met young people who hadn't eaten anything in several days. When someone doesn't eat for days, it doesn't take a lot of imagination to see why Jim grabbed a disgusting ear of corn. Soup kitchens and food pantries are in every major city as well as many small towns around the world today. The issues that Jim faced when he left home are issues many of our young people face every day.

Two years ago, in the area where I live, a local charity was looking for people to help fund hygiene kits for high school students. The shocking statistic that more than one thousand high school students were homeless in our area caught me completely off guard. Their families had fallen on hard times and needed help. The issue of homelessness is everywhere, even if you don't see it. The homeless are in every city and in every community no matter the size. Homelessness is a complicated problem around the world and not everyone who finds themselves homeless is at fault. You can find Jim everywhere. Jim's choices came with consequences and often those consequences provide very difficult life lessons.

The basic problem is that each of us, despite our circumstances, is a wretch. You can be wearing the finest clothes or eating at the finest restaurants. You may not be living on the street or squandering your life on drugs or wild living, but you're no different from anyone else. Even if you change the words to *Amazing Grace* or believe you were never a wretch, the condition of your soul means you need a Savior.

Because we're all in the same predicament, the four things God does not know will apply to each of us. I admit I didn't create these. As a matter of fact, I received them from an unlikely source. I wrote these down during an Air Force briefing on diversity.

In 2004, I received orders to go to Ramstein Air Base, in Germany and during that tour I was selected to attend the Senior Non-Commissioned Officer Academy. This course is the third level of professional military education for Air Force enlisted members. The school, located at Maxwell Air Force Base Gunter Annex in Alabama, prepares senior non-commissioned officers

(NCO) to take on greater leadership roles within the enlisted force. This course challenges selected senior NCOs to think critically on a more strategic level. The military faces many challenging environments and this course addresses a wide variety of subjects. One of those topics was "Diversity as a Leadership Strategy".

The military brings people from every corner of society and begins molding them into a unified fighting machine. Not only do we need to ensure military leaders are capable of such a task, but they must also be able to do so without being influenced by their own biases. This is no easy task, but most of our military leaders do it well every day.

Returning to the subject, the diversity topic featured a guest speaker from Chicago, Dr. Samuel Betances. His excellent presentation centered on how we all have a responsibility to keep our differences from negatively impacting our workplace. Even years later I remember many of his points and still have the notes I took. Early in his presentation, he mentioned four spiritual points. I quickly wrote them down, leaned over to a friend and said, "That will preach."

As we look at each of these four points, you'll see I'm not stating anything theologically inaccurate. I believe in the sovereignty of God and that He is all powerful, all knowing, and all present. I also believe in the free will of man. Those mysteries are powerful truths, but I hope to show that there are truly some things God does not know.

Each truth stands on its own, but the way I'll develop them, they build on each other. One truth leads to the next and strengthens the foundation of the previous one. Every time I review these truths I'm reminded that they apply not only to new Christians, but also to all Christians.

The parable of the Prodigal Son is more than a story of how

a lost son came home. I firmly believe this is a parable for all of us. A new Christian can see how his life used to be and how his Heavenly Father has compassion for him. But, the Christian who has been faithful in His service for decades can especially benefit from the message as it applies to Believers. All Believers will see the need for a Savior who can, and will, offer renewal and help us walk a life of faith even during the most difficult times.

Without a doubt, the parable is a reflection of each of us and how we're in need of forgiveness and compassion. As written by John Newton, we are all in need of God's amazing grace. Jim is a part of us and how we wander away from God's desire for our lives. I'm a sinner saved by the grace of God and through the atoning work of Jesus Christ as well as the regeneration of the Holy Spirit, I'm a better man. But, it's vital to realize Jesus didn't come to earth to die and make us better men and women. Jesus didn't come to change me from a bad man to a good one. His mission was more important. Jesus came to transform me from a dead person to a living one; to bring us all from death to life.

I've been following Jesus for more than 40 years and feel I'm a fairly good man. I also realize I'm not much different than the person who doesn't believe. And, sometimes I'm worse. I know many men who are better all-around examples than I am. Throughout Scripture there are many examples of people who've started a walk of faith but faltered and ultimately didn't finish well. Let's look at several examples before we go further. The following examples happen to fit well into our story since we're looking at the dynamics of a father-son relationship.

David came from very humble beginnings and ultimately became King of Israel. To this day, he is revered as Israel's greatest King as well as a significant historical figure. As the youngest of eight boys in his family, he displayed humility and never seemed to force his way into the leadership role. Even as a young man he showed extraordinary courage and faith. After he killed the giant, Goliath, he was hailed as a hero of the battle. He was selected and anointed as king by the Prophet Samuel and soon took his place on the throne after the death of Saul, the prior king.

David was called a man after God's own heart. He had a talent for music and poetry, writing many of the Psalms. However, David still committed some incredibly evil deeds. He's famous for lax treatment of his military responsibilities, committing adultery, and ultimately conspiring to commit murder. There is no better example of how precarious a walk of faith can become. David did well when he walked closely with God, but as soon as he stepped away from God, drawn by his own lusts and sinful desires, his life spiraled out of control.

Before his death, David anointed Solomon as king to ensure his son would ascend the throne. Solomon is known for his wisdom. When God asked King Solomon what he desired, Solomon requested the wisdom to be a good ruler. Examples of his wisdom are found in the books of Proverbs, Ecclesiastes, and the Song of Solomon. However, Solomon is an excellent example of someone who started well but didn't finish that way. His foreign wives and concubines eventually brought about his moral downfall and his heart was led away from God.

Our spiritual journey is often a rocky road. Some days we're full of faith, but it doesn't take much to knock us back down where we doubt and question. Just like David and Solomon, my spiritual journey is on thin ice when I venture away from God to seek after my own desires. Even the best of my intentions, if not aligned with God's word, will lead to sin. Despite believing I'm a good man, I must never forget I'm human and capable of having evil desires reside in my heart. And according to Matthew 15:18-20, it's those things that defile me and carry severe consequences.

On the first blank page in my Bible, I've written quotes I want to remember. I don't know their sources or the reason I saved each one, but one reminds me that my walk of faith can be fragile. At the top of the page I recorded this quote from Kaj Munk (1898 - 1944), a Danish pastor who was martyred for speaking against the Nazis during World War II:

> "All here are Christians, to be sure, but beware, not too much."

What does God not know? The first truth establishes the foundation we must build on.

Chapter Ten:

God Doesn't Know a Sin
He won't Forgive

G od doesn't know a sin He won't forgive.

In our story, Jim ventures off and squanders his wealth on wild living. There's no doubt Jim did things his parents would never approve. Although we're not given any indication of the father's faith, the way both sons reacted indicates there was a firm sense of right and wrong in the house. Jim's own confession to his father provides evidence he was raised in a home where the difference between right and wrong was taught in an environment of faith. He had some understanding of sacred matters. When Jesus told the parable, Jim admitted the obvious to his father, "I have sinned against Heaven and against you" (Mark 15:18). The older son loudly protested the party by stating, "This son of yours who has squandered your property with prostitutes…" (Mark 15:30). It is clear both boys knew the difference between acceptable and unacceptable behavior.

The father wasn't blind to his son's deeds and didn't excuse them. Over the course of time, Jim's behavior was a topic of family conversation. If his father was influential, even if only in his own local area, he would have heard travelers' gossip. He may have asked them to secretly check on his son's welfare. Of course, such a report would also include news of his behavior. When the news arrived, the discussion around the dinner table was disheartening, but at least they had news. When I was overseas, my phone would occasionally ring and a parent would ask if I could get a message to their child. As an NCO, I always located the son or daughter, passed on the message, and urged them to call home. I'm sure if the father in our story had any contacts in the city, he'd say, "Hey, if you get the chance would you check up on my boy?"

When I first left home, my Mom and Dad made me promise to call at least once a month. For the most part, I kept that promise. Before cell phones were widely available they told me to call collect, even when I was overseas. They never complained about the phone bill, although I'm sure it was astronomical. Why did they want word on how and what I was doing? Because parents care about their children and even if the news isn't great at least they know.

When Jim arrived home, his father unashamedly celebrated his son's return. Nowhere does Scripture indicate the father looked disapprovingly at his youngest son. It doesn't mean the father approved of his son's behavior. It does mean the father was overjoyed to have his son home alive. However, in our text, we get the sense that Jim is acutely ashamed of what he did. He's aware his behavior brought discredit to both his family and to God. He's especially sensitive to the damage to his father's reputation. Without hesitation Jim admitted he has grievously sinned. Although the parable lacks the details, it does say Jim spent his inheritance on wild living. It doesn't take much imagination to realize how stupid a young man can be, especially a young man with a great deal of money. "Father," Jim said, "I've sinned against Heaven and against you. I'm no longer worthy to be called your son." That's quite a statement coming from a young man in his position. Jim has come a long way.

But, the reaction of Jim's father is totally different from what the son expected. Instead of recriminations, he commanded a servant to bring a robe, a ring, and sandals to make his son presentable. At this point, Jim was anything but presentable. Not only did his father see him from a distance, he likely was able to smell his son from a long way off too. If anyone has ever worked on a farm, you're aware it's dirty work. Jim had to reek. If Jim's boss wasn't concerned with the food he ate, it's likely he was just as unconcerned about Jim's clothes or personal hygiene. Despite Jim's stench, his father ran to him, hugged him, and kissed him.

In the early 1990's, at the start of the first Gulf War, I was stationed at the twin bases of RAF Bentwaters and RAF Woodbridge in the United Kingdom. Shortly after Iraq invaded Kuwait, I received deployment orders to support a search and rescue mission in Turkey. Our unit's mission was to locate and rescue any pilots who were or might have been shot down over western Iraq. The chaplain and I flew with the Special Operations Squadron to Incirlik Air Base in Turkey. Our final destination was a small base in the mountains near the Iraqi border. It was a "bare base" location, meaning we had to establish the base from nothing. When I arrived, there were no showers, laundry facilities, dining facilities, or even tents. When the ministry team stepped off the plane, the chaplain was number 46 and I was number 47 on the ground. The base ultimately grew to nearly 500 personnel, but those first few weeks were filled with a lot of work and not a lot of hygiene.

Due to an urgent family situation in the States, the commander granted me a week of emergency leave. My instructions were to get home, put the family on a flight, and return. I flew via a C-130 cargo plane back to Incirlik where I waited several hours to board another C-130 for the long flight to the United Kingdom. It was well past midnight when I landed at RAF Mildenhall and took a nearly two-hour taxi ride back to my home base. The taxi dropped me at the gate and I walked home at "o-dark-thirty," as the saying goes.

Because everyone was asleep, I knocked on the dark door, waited, and after a few minutes knocked again. After asking who was there through the upstairs window, my wife realized I was home and ran downstairs. She threw open the front door, and in tears, reached out to give me a hug but stopped just as her arms were about to wrap around my neck. "What's that smell?", she asked. Unfortunately, it was me. Hard work, diesel fuel, mud, and no showers had created a less than delightful aroma. With tears still streaming down her face, but now with a wide smile, my bride said, "Go take a shower and then I'll give you a proper welcome home greeting."

In our story, Jim's father was so overcome with compassion he didn't stop in mid-hug. Despite his son's prepared speech, the father welcomed him back into the family as if nothing had changed. Why? The answer is found in the second half of Luke 15:20. This verse states, "But while he was still a long way off, his father saw him and was filled with compassion for him…" The reason is simple to understand. The father saw his son while he was still a long distance away and ran to meet him. He recognized his son long before he was home. Maybe it was the way his son walked. We don't know, but no matter how, the father knew it was his son. And, he was filled with compassion for his son. The father's compassion is the key element. He willingly overlooked Jim's outward appearance. Jim knew he wasn't worthy. He readily admitted his wrongdoing and was willing to pay the price for his transgressions. He accepted his sin was egregious and was willing to face the consequences. But, his father's compassion looked past all of it and embraced him just as he was.

Compassion isn't ignorance of sins, nor does it ignore bad behavior. Compassion looks past those things and sees a person's value. Compassion embraces the worst offender and offers love and acceptance without reservation. Compassion offers forgiveness freely as it brushes aside wrongs committed in ignorance or selfishness. Despite the wrongs, our Heavenly Father has compassion on us and is willing to freely forgive all our sins.

While Jim was giving his speech, his father commanded a robe to be put on him and sandals for his feet. "Put the family ring on his finger" the father commanded. "Start the preparations, kill the fattest calf we have." That illustrates the unashamed compassion and love a father has for his son. He sees past the wrongs and freely forgives. The truth of forgiveness isn't a truth rendered in a single Scripture verse. It's woven throughout the Bible.

In Colossians 2:13, we read that Christ forgave all our sins. "You were dead in your sins and in the uncircumcision of your sinful nature, God made you alive with Christ. He forgave us ALL our sins." The emphasis is mine.

In Ephesians 1:7 we read, "In Him we have redemption through His blood, the forgiveness of sins, in accordance with the riches of God's grace."

God's forgiveness isn't something we earn or deserve. He gives it freely as often as we need in accordance with the riches of His grace. If mercy isn't getting what you deserve, grace is getting what you don't deserve. And we all need His forgiveness, often.

God does not know a sin He won't forgive.

However, there's one important exception. Before we continue, I should briefly discuss the one sin Jesus states will not be forgiven.

Matthew 12:31 reads: "And so I tell you, every sin and blasphemy will be forgiven men, but the blasphemy against the Spirit will not be forgiven." And, in Mark 3:28-29, Scripture states, "I tell you the truth, all the sins and blasphemies of men will be forgiven them. But whoever blasphemes against the Holy Spirit will never be forgiven; he is guilty of eternal sin."

I've been in Baptist, Catholic, Pentecostal, and Liturgical circles where we've discussed this one unforgivable sin. I don't remember all the discussions and debates, but I know there are various opinions. Some definitions of this particular sin were simple, others thought-provoking, while some were more complicated depending on denominational doctrine. Although the sin against the Spirit is not the subject of this book, I feel I need to address it from this layman's perspective.

I've had many Christians come to me in tears and admit they believed they sinned against God's Spirit and felt they were now lost. They'd sinned against God, were confronted by their sin, and now faced the consequences. I think about how lost Jim felt when he first attempted to express his sin to his father. Jim's internal conflict was intense. He was overcome by his father's reaction but tormented because he believed his actions made him unworthy. This must be how these Christians felt, but I don't believe these individuals committed the unforgiveable sin against God's Spirit.

There are two points I'd like to address about blaspheming the Holy Spirt. First, we know forgiveness is an essential part of redemption. Without God's forgiveness a person is eternally lost. I don't know how prevalent the sin against the Spirit is. However, when a person commits the unforgiveable sin, they no longer feel conviction from the Spirit or the pull of God's grace. A person cannot respond to God's invitation if the Holy Spirit no longer calls. When God withdraws His Spirit from a person, that person can no longer experience redemption. I doubt this person would cry over their sin because they would no longer feel the convicting power of the Holy Spirit.

Second, when a person regretfully confesses sin, they are experiencing the convicting power of the Holy Spirit and there is hope for redemption. They may feel they've committed the unpardonable sin, but if they feel conviction, that fact indicates they haven't. Many tears have been shed over sin and when there is genuine sorrow forgiveness is close by. Each of us faces temptation when, "by his own evil desire, he is dragged away and enticed. Then, after desire is conceived, it gives birth to sin; and sin, when it is full-grown, gives birth to death" (James 1:14-15). Christians have an ongoing internal fight with our flesh because we allow ourselves to be drawn away and enticed. But God's Spirit calls to us and convicts us of our sin. Conviction by the Holy Spirit isn't pleasant, but it's necessary for our spiritual maturity. For those who feel they are so far away from God they can't be redeemed, nothing is further from the truth. If you still feel the convicting power of the Holy Spirit, rest assured, God has not withdrawn His Spirit. As long as God calls to an individual there is hope for redemption. As long as God calls, they are not eternally lost.

I realize using only these two points: the Holy Spirit is withdrawn from someone or He is constantly working and leading a person into God's truth, is a simplistic look at a complex theological principle. From my perspective, it clarifies a necessary point of view. I know some will have differing opinions, but I hope we can agree on this: If a person feels the tug of conviction, the desire to ask for forgiveness, or longs to find the missing piece, they realize God doesn't know a sin He won't forgive.

I've had individuals tearfully state there is no possibility God would accept them back again. "You have no idea the things I've done," they cry. The cry is the same from all prodigals, but the response from God is also always the same. He doesn't know a sin He won't forgive.

The day started sunny and bright but soon became overcast and depressing. I found myself sitting next to Jennifer, a young lady whose life was in turmoil. She was divorced, unemployed, and facing significant consequences for a variety of legal actions stemming from an assortment of crimes she committed. If I said her life was difficult, it would be an understatement; chaos swirled around her. However, her life hadn't always been this way. In the past, it had held promise, hope, and purpose. On this particular day, she sat in my passenger seat as we drove through town. Our conversation started with small talk, but soon became more personal. As the conversation became more intense, she confessed her life was a mess and she was unsure how it could all work out.

"I know, I know," she would repeat when she described a choice she made and I commented it wasn't the best option.

When we arrived at our destination, I parked and turned off the engine. Our conversation turned to the spiritual matters she wrestled with. She was familiar with faith but like other prodigals she slowly wandered away over time.

"That faith stuff works for you, but apparently not for me. You know I was raised in church, guess somewhere along the way I took a wrong turn," she admitted looking down at her hands folded in her lap, avoiding my gaze.

"You know, God is in the same place. He will welcome you back," I replied.

Her head shot up and as tears filled her eyes she shook her head. "No. That isn't possible. Do you know what I've done? Do you have any idea what a mess I've made of my life?"

"God knows what you've done and He's more than willing to take you back." I stated firmly but gently. "Not only will He take you back, but He'll also forgive everything."

Her tears overflowed and, as they ran down her face, she wiped them away with the back of her hand. "You mean to tell me I can go back to when I was 14 years old?" When I nodded she said, "I'll have to think about this." She got out of the car and went on her way.

I've heard sentiments such as, "My sin is too great for even the God of the Universe to overlook" more times than I can count. Many of us look at our wrongs and realize those wrongs are mounting higher every day. We can't imagine God would forgive and accept us when the reality is we have difficulty forgiving ourselves. God has no such difficulty.

Like all prodigals, it was difficult for this young woman to grasp the depth of God's love and His willingness to forgive her. He truly would accept her just as she was. Prodigals recognize their true condition for they clearly see the warts, blemishes, and scars. The concept of total forgiveness is difficult to grasp and, in many cases, nearly impossible to embrace.

I had more conversations with Jennifer. As time passed, her drug and legal issues as well as relationship woes took a dreadful turn and one night she tried to end her life. This attempt resulted in a severe brain injury. Her life hung in the balance with little hope from the medical experts. Her story is an amazing one of a life lost to despair that finally became a miraculous recovery over the course of years. Her triumph was like hearing your baby's first words or watching their first unsteady steps. She learned to walk and feed herself without assistance, two tasks doctors believed were beyond her ability. Hers was a life lost and then born again.

Our paths cross daily but also at church each Sunday. She'll tell you of her desire to live a life free of all the old baggage. I'm positive it's not always easy as anyone who decides to embrace this new life will understand. There will be setbacks and mistakes, and times the Holy Spirit will convict her of sin. She also understands going back to a bankrupt life is simple, living the life of a Christian woman is more difficult. However, she now lives a life free from past sins. Her story is one of tragedy, of wasted potential, and great heartache when life collapsed in a terrible chain of events but rose from the ashes for another opportunity, for a second chance.

Imagine the worst a human could be guilty of and I'll show you someone who did the same thing and still experienced forgiveness. It doesn't matter what you've done. It doesn't matter how far away you are. God is still calling you today.

The foundation of the Prodigal Son parable is that God is compassionate and doesn't know a sin He won't forgive. The good news is God's grace and forgiveness know no boundaries. Those attributes are all part of God's nature and He's always true to His nature. Despite his condition, Jim realized his father's compassion would encompass him and not hold anything against him, just as God's forgiveness is available to us, no matter what we've done.

I've met prodigals who willingly accept that God freely forgives, but it's as if they expect God to take a nonchalant view of their sin. I've heard preachers teach that God's nature will forgive in all cases. They teach when you die it will turn out fine because God is compassionate and will forgive everyone. That belief isn't based on a comprehensive viewpoint of Scripture.

God's forgiveness is complete, but we humans have trouble forgiving others. Most of us have heard the old saying, "I may forgive, but I won't forget." I know many who won't even consider forgiving someone else as they hold onto a grudge like there's no tomorrow. To make the matter of forgiveness even more complex, we also have trouble forgiving ourselves. We often lament about things we've done in the past. Since we know how difficult forgiveness can be, can we comprehend that it's not going to be automatic when we stand before God?

What does God not know? God doesn't know a sin He won't forgive. This truth is our first building block. Since God's forgiveness is all-inclusive, He doesn't have difficulty with the offense no matter how heinous we may think it is. He also doesn't have difficulty putting it and leaving it in the past, where it's forgotten.

With the understanding of the first truth, the second illustrates our responsibility. What do we do to make the first truth a reality in our lives?

Chapter Eleven:

God Doesn't Know a Better Time To Repent

S ince God doesn't know a sin He won't forgive, we now turn our attention to the second truth which puts the first into practice.

The second truth is: *God doesn't know a better time to repent.*

We all have our favorite Scriptures. I know people who have a "life verse", a portion of Scripture that guides and anchors their daily lives. There are many reasons why some Scriptures hold a special place in our lives. Some Scriptures seem to stand out to us. In my opinion, Luke 15:17 is one of those. I've read it more than a hundred times. It doesn't matter how often I've read it, when I see those words they jump off of the page. Let me show you what I mean. Verse 17 begins, "When he came to his senses…" My heart skips a beat when I read that amazing verse.

I picture Jim feeding the pigs. Dumping the spoiled food from big buckets into the troughs. As he's carrying the buckets, the contents slosh over the sides onto his hands and clothes. In the summer heat, maggots and flies crawl and buzz everywhere and are overwhelming. Jim smells the same as the slop. But, because it's been weeks since he had a bath, he no longer notices the stench.

You know things are bad, when the rotten food you're feeding the pigs looks edible, so much so that you're thinking of reaching into the bucket and grabbing that half-eaten ear of corn. If you did, you'd quickly wipe off the bugs and, when you've finished, it would fill your stomach for a little while. You ignore you're a mess. You grab another bucket and move to the next trough.

Not only did he have a distinct aroma, Jim must have also been a miserable sight with his hair and beard matted with slop and manure. His fine city clothes were reduced to less than filthy rags on his emaciated frame. In rags, barefoot, and constantly hungry, this was Jim's daily routine. Then one day, just as he reached for another morsel from the vile bucket, he came to his senses. In that instant, he realized he was a wretch, but he also knew he didn't have to stay in that condition. Hope, vacant just moments before, surged through him.

I picture him standing ankle-deep in pig manure, holding a half-eaten corn cob. As he wipes it with his filthy shirt, he spies worms are also sharing his dinner. At that moment he remembers the nightly meals his father's servants received.

He decides he wants to go home and realizes, in that moment, home is far better than here. He fails to see the irony that he once hated home and longed for the big city, but now his view is completely reversed. He longs for home and knows his father was correct. He comes to his senses and is sorry for the mess he made of his life and for the sins that have separated him from his father and his God. He begins to rehearse the speech showing his remorse. His words are inadequate, but his remorse is indeed genuine.

I'll assume while some of us may have been in situations similar to Jim's, none of us have been eating pig slop. We might also make the assumption that someone who's fallen on hard times has also fallen away from God, but we'd be wrong. Many famous Biblical characters did without the basic comforts of life. We must never forget someone's condition in this life doesn't necessarily relate to their condition in the next. It may be the opposite. It's been said a person with all his needs met has a more difficult time realizing he needs a Savior. A person who comes face-to-face with his failings may have less difficulty understanding his true spiritual condition. However, a person who thinks his wealth is sufficient might deny the truth of his wretchedness. Even the person who believes he's a good person may not realize his spirit is bankrupt.

Your position in life doesn't signify your relationship with God. Most of us misunderstand how our right standing with God is determined. You may be rich or poor, homeless or reside in a mansion. You may be of any race or ethnicity. Your spiritual condition isn't reflective of your situation, but of your heart. If you're a wretch covered in pig slop, you're far away from God. If you're a wretch sitting in a twenty-first floor corner office wearing a three-piece suit, you're also far away from God. Those two spiritual conditions are identical. It's easy to make the mistake of judging someone's spiritual condition on what we see. The person who's generous to a fault may also be incorrectly judged as being spiritually whole, when in fact they may not be. The truth is it doesn't matter if we have much or if we have nothing.

When a person comes to the Cross, they leave all they have or all they lack behind. Both, the list of life's accomplishments and the list of wasted opportunities fall aside on the way to Calvary.

The individual with a large bank account stands side-by-side with the financially inept. They are equal in the light of the Cross. When we approach the Cross all we are, all we've done, and all our good falls away and we all stand on level ground. In life very little is equal. Each person has different talents and different opportunities. Some have an easier road to success, while others have an uphill struggle. But, when we stand before the Cross, we are all equal. Only twice in our lives will we stand 100 percent equal with each other. The first is before the Cross. When we stand before the Cross, everything is obliterated and we are left with all we have to offer, ourselves and our sin. The second is when we stand before God after our death.

We don't stand with our good works. Nothing we do can ever pay for the forgiveness we desire and need. The accountant can't justify stealing a million dollars because he volunteered his time at the local food bank. The doctor can't boast of the fifty patients he successfully treated to justify the one that died from his negligence. Each and every one of us must realize no matter where we live, how we dress, or the car we drive, our spiritual condition is in a wretched state.

Over the years I've asked many prodigals this question, "If you were to stand before God, why would he let you into Heaven?" The answers run the gamut of the human condition. I've had some say they aren't worthy. Others flatly state they are a good person and that's enough. Some state they gave money to charity, haven't stolen as much as the next person, or are no worse than anyone else. All their reasoning falls aside as they approach the Cross. We can't earn our way into Heaven. Until we come to our senses, we remain prodigals. When Jim stopped long enough to hear his heart's cry, he finally came to his senses. We all need to come to our senses and decide if we will go to the Father.

When did Jim become his father's son again? He was always his father's son, he simply didn't know it. He could have gone home any time, but he considered that door closed. Figuratively, Jim became his father's son again when he came to his senses. The circumstances hadn't changed. Jim was still at the same location and, at least for the moment, in the same mess as he was moments before. But at the moment he came to his senses, he was his father's son again. All it took was for Jim to repent.

In Second Corinthians 6:2, the second half of the verse says, "I tell you, now is the time of God's favor, now is the day of salvation." The right time is today, not tomorrow when you've cleaned yourself up enough and not when you've perfected your "welcome home" speech or when you've set your affairs in order. Today is the day when you should decide.

In the second chapter of the book of Acts, the Apostle Peter stood before a crowd and preached one of the greatest sermons in Christian history. This was the first sermon of the infant Christian Church. Peter emphatically stated that the crowd, with the help of evil men, had killed Jesus. However, not a single man in the crowd literally fashioned a crown of thorns and jammed it onto Jesus's head. No one in the crowd disagreed with Peter even though none had lifted the hammer or driven the nails into His hands and feet. Verse thirty-seven reads, "When the people heard this, they were cut to the heart and said to Peter and the other apostles, 'Brothers, what shall we do?' (Acts 2:37)

The people who heard Peter came to their senses. They came face-to-face with their sin and were cut to the heart. They were faced with what they'd done and were forced to acknowledge the fact they killed the Son of God. They were from all walks of life. From different cities, as well as different countries. Even though they had diverse cultures and traditions when they were confronted with the truth, a decision had to be made. They cried out to the apostles for a solution to mitigate their guilt. Peter was concise when he gave them the solution. "Repent," he said. Repentance is a sorrowful turning away from sin and a decision to live your life for God.

If God doesn't know a sin He won't forgive, He also doesn't know a better time to repent. The first step back to God is the simple act of repentance. Repentance may be simple, but it's not easy. We often struggle with repentance but when we take this initial step it's life-changing.

I met a young mother with two children who told the story of her conversion to Christianity. She was raised in Thailand and each year her parents gathered the entire family to go worship in the mountains. As she told her emotional story her heavy Thai accent became more pronounced. It had been many years, but as she told the story I could tell it was as if it had happened yesterday.

Every year the family would gather at a mountain temple where they offered incense and prayers over the course of a few days. As she got older, she began to question her faith. She talked of the inner struggle as well as the struggle with family traditions. One night, as the sun began to set, she walked through the manicured temple grounds and looked out over the forest below. The canopy of trees below looked so solid she felt she could walk along the treetops. The sun was setting and the brilliant purple and red sky was breathtaking. Tears welled up in her eyes when she said to me, "As I gazed at that sunset, I knew. I knew there was something more than offering incense in a temple. I looked up at that painted sky and asked God to show me the right way to Him."

Shortly after the family returned home, a new Christian mission opened offering to teach English to anyone willing to learn. Her sister refused to go unless she went too. One day the teacher told the students about Jesus Christ and how He would forgive them if they simply asked.

A smile replaced her tears as she exuberantly continued, "As soon as I heard the Gospel story, I knew this was the answer to my prayers. My heart jumped within me and I wasted no time asking for forgiveness." She came to her senses and was never the same again. I'll never forget her story because it was dramatic and life-changing.

However, sometimes conversion isn't the result of years of searching, longing for the truth, as it was in the young mother's case. Sometimes it's a quiet request to God to come make us different. And the results can be sudden and equally dramatic.

In mid-1982, orders arrived telling me Uncle Sam was sending me from RAF Lakenheath in the United Kingdom to Plattsburgh, New York. I soon met Steve and we quickly became good friends. Although we worked together, our faith proved to be the major connection. Steve told me he'd recently become a Christian. We were as different as we could be, but because of that faith connection we created a friendship that's lasted more than thirty years.

Prior to his conversion, Steve had a reputation as someone who loved to party and wasn't afraid to get into an occasional fight. One of his "finest" moments happened on one of the town's main streets. Steve had been drinking and got into an altercation with an individual on the sidewalk in front of a furniture store. The altercation escalated and finally Steve picked the man up, hoisted him overhead, and threw him through the plate glass window onto a bedroom display. Years later, he recounted that story with regret. But, the one story he loved to share was of his conversion.

It was a quiet conversion with little fanfare, but the change in his life was dramatic. Just before my arrival, Steve had noticed another Airman in the barracks. Steve described him this way, "He was different. He wasn't like the rest of us, but I didn't know why." He watched the Airman for awhile but couldn't figure him out. He was stumped. One day Steve walked up to him and asked, "What's wrong with you? Why are you different?"

The reply was short and to the point, "I'm a Christian." That concise answer accomplished its purpose. Later that night, Steve turned his gaze toward Heaven and said, "God, if You're up there and can hear me, make me like him."

I haven't had the privilege of meeting the man who was such an example for Steve, but his life served as a beacon for at least one man in the cold north woods. Steve's life suddenly changed and every person in the 380th Security Police Squadron who knew Steve witnessed the dramatic difference.

Steve would say he'd been a wretch for years and the change he experienced happened overnight. There's only one explanation. Steve came to his senses. He was an example of a young Airman with a future. His uniform was always pressed and looking sharp. He knew his job and had the skills to do it well. But, it didn't change the fact he was a wretch. Then one night, a simple prayer of "make me like him" and his whole life changed. At that moment, Steve became a son of the Father and began to experience a life-changing transformation. That was Steve's moment of repentance. Steve would tell you he had a long list of wrongs, but in that moment, they vanished. Because God did not know one of Steve's sins that couldn't be forgiven and, as Steve found out, there was no better time to repent.

Repentance is a neglected spiritual practice. I've talked with many Christians who feel repentance pertains only to new converts.

More established believers sometimes feel the act of repentance doesn't pertain to them any longer. However, repentance is vital to a healthy Christian life of continued growth and maturity.

For many years after I became a Christian, most church services were followed by an altar call. To clarify this term for our discourse, the altar is the area in front of the first row of seating but before the pulpit. Before closing the service, the minister would ask anyone who wanted to accept the Lord or needed prayer to come to the altar. Since the Sunday morning service often focused on salvation, an altar call provided an opportunity to invite Jesus into a person's life. Sunday night services, however, were primarily for believers already walking with God. The sermons offered more of a variety of topics. The altar call was also significantly different.

On Sunday night the pastor would invite anyone to the altar for prayer for any issue. Often, that invitation would be like a mini-sermon. The pastor focused on the subject of his sermon and then called those who were struggling with this particular issue to come forward and repent. The practice of going forward for prayer on Sunday nights helped shape my view that repentance should be regular, consistent, and heartfelt.

When I joined the Air Force I'd been a Christian for many years. However, I had a lot of growing up to do. Not only did I need to grow into a responsible adult but I also needed to grow up spiritually. An integral part of maturing as a Christian was the time I spent repenting at the altar for bad behavior. The sermon might bring a sin to my attention or a subject in Bible study highlighted an area where I was lacking. At work or during a basketball game one of my brothers would point out a behavior that didn't bring glory to God. No matter where I was or what I was doing, the Holy Spirit always brought those attitudes to my attention. Sunday nights held a special place in my week. I could kneel at the altar and set things right.

After nearly six years as an Air Force Security Policeman, I was accepted into the Chaplain Corps as a Chaplain Assistant. Those first six years established the foundation for the rest of my career. The irregular shifts made it difficult to know whether I was coming or going. Even if my shift ended early Sunday morning, I took the time to attend church.

After a long week, I was in church one Sunday morning. The opportunity to slow down for the next hour was a relief. On this particular day, two young Airmen came into the worship service after it started. They were in uniform and one thing seemed clear, they looked to be under stress. They nervously took seats three or four pews in front of me. After the song service, the pastor placed his Bible on the podium and opened it indicating it was time for his sermon. One of the young men stood up and loudly said, "Excuse me sir, I hate to interrupt." The pastor looked up and asked what his question was. The man replied, "I don't have a question, sir. I need to repent." The second man stood up and exclaimed, "Me too. I'm with him." The pastor, closed his Bible and said, "Then come on up, let's take care of this right now."

After praying with these young men, the pastor stated that their actions were all the sermon we needed for the day. He invited the rest of the congregation to put the practice of repentance into action. These two men, no matter what their issues, understood that God didn't know a better time to repent.

Times have changed. Many churches don't have time for altar calls because multiple services limit the available time between services. There are a lot of parts to reset in order to be ready for the next group. Now a person who feels compelled to give their life to Christ raises a hand, we pray, and then move on. A person who feels the full weight of conviction is often in the same boat, if they're even given the opportunity to acknowledge it with a raised hand.

I fully understand the complicated dynamics of multiple services churches face. Many churches have compensated for this new predicament by carving out time for prayer during services. One church I attended for years, has an altar call during a special part of the song service. Another church invites people to come forward for prayer just before the end of the service. Another has the practice of praying at the altar when they sing at the start of the service. Even though many churches have found ways to fill this need, I wonder if it's as effective as it used to be.

The lack of Sunday evening services also adds to the dilemma. Often, there is no time to pray and steel our heart toward convictions. When a Christian is confronted with sin, the best thing to do is repent. It doesn't have to be in a church setting. The most important thing to remember is that when we become aware of sin in our lives, we need to repent. However, it's often in a church setting, away from the demands of work and family that our hearts are sensitive and our minds open to the work of the Holy Spirit.

There should be a stark distinction between Christian and non-Christian homes. Our lives should reflect our faith. When lives don't, we need to recognize it and repent. Since repentance is a sorrowful turning away from sin, we should do it often and it should have an impact on how we live. We often dabble in our sin and never really confront it. We justify our behavior as our right, point out it isn't that bad, or blame it on someone else. But when our sin confronts us, we should crucify it once and for all. Instead of attempting to justify our behavior, we should embrace the viewpoint that there isn't any excuse for bad behavior. We just need to repent.

In the mid to late 1980's, I heard about a marriage seminar offered at a local evangelical church. It was scheduled for three nights and since it sounded interesting, I signed up. There's some significant dialogue I remember from that seminar. The seminar leaders stated the divorce rate was 52 percent or nearly one out of every two marriages in the general population. They pointed out that statistics for second and third marriages are even worse. But, they did have some good news. If you attended church once a week as a couple your odds went from one in two to one in fifty-two or less than 2 percent. In addition, they pointed out it didn't matter which church you attended, as long as you did it together.

The last set of statistics they shared indicated that if you attended an evangelical church the numbers in your favor were even higher. The average rose from 52 percent for the general population, to less than 2 percent if you attended church as a couple, to less than one-tenth of 1 percent if you attended an evangelical church.

I realize there are some problems with these statistics. When you use statistics to support a point they should be verifiable, accurate, and current. I don't believe the statistics I'm using here meet any of those criteria. First, I don't have a citation to verify accuracy. I don't remember whether or not the presenters identified their sources. Second, I'm recalling this seminar from the 1980's. What else do I remember from a seminar I attended nearly forty years ago? I remember several things, but the most important is that overall it wasn't very beneficial. Why am I recalling a seminar I didn't like and quoting statistics that may or may not be accurate? I want to compare the 1980 seminar statistics with the following current statistics.

Divorcestatistics.info cites various studies and data that report the current overall divorce rate is about 50 percent. The website defines divorce rates by the number of times someone was married. First marriages ended in divorce between 41 and 50 percent of the time. For second marriages, 60 to 67 percent end in divorce. The percentage increases to an astounding 73 to 74 percent for third time marriages. [6]

The Barna Research Group reported there is no statistical difference in the divorce rates for born again Christians when compared to the general population. As a matter of fact, according to the Barna study, the divorce rate in the general population was 2 percent lower than among born again Christians. [7]

Could things have really changed that drastically from the 1980's? Is it really possible the overall church divorce rate is identical to that of the general population? Research indicates some disagreements with the cited 50 percent divorce rate statistics. The Barna study indicates an overall lower percentage rate of divorce, about half of the often-quoted 50 percent rate. [8] The percentage rate is not the issue. Although some may debate if the rate of divorce is higher or lower in the church today, it's this debate that focuses on the issue. The fact that we even debate whether the divorce rates are the same or possibly higher among Christians when compared to the general population, shows how radically the demographics have changed.

The argument isn't whether or not professing Christians should have a lower divorce rate. Divorce is a painful experience for families, including children. Divorcestatistics.info states children from divorced parents are four-times more likely to divorce than children from couples who don't divorce. [9] Hopefully, families experiencing the pain of divorce look to the church for help.

If the divorce rate is higher in the church, it wouldn't be a surprise. The church is a reflection of society and we frequently see the impact of society in and on the church. If you picked an area of dysfunction including anger, greed, lust, etc., you'd see how the church exhibits some of the same dysfunction at the same level as the general population. Depending on the statistics, in some cases, the level of Christian dysfunction may be even higher.

This is the point. Perhaps today's church needs to take time to repent. Husbands and wives need to sit down, get before God and repent. I'm not throwing any stones. My life is not held up as a shining light. I'm not ignoring my need to repent by pointing the finger at anyone. I'm fully aware of my failings as a father, husband, son, friend, and Christian because I've failed to repent and submit my life to God. In an effort to be transparent, I willingly admit I've failed more times than I care to think. I don't make excuses for my bad behavior. When I do wrong I recognize it as sin and it must be eradicated from my life. I'm no different from the next man. I can't do it on my own. I still sin and am in need of a Savior.

Recently I heard a story illustrating how vital repentance is in a Christian's life. A couple was celebrating their wedding anniversary. The husband pulled out all the stops by purchasing flowers, a romantic dinner by candlelight, and taking a moonlit walk. The husband wrapped his arms around his wife and as he prepared to kiss her she said, "I'm sorry, but I'm not sure I want to be married any longer." The husband listened as the wife expressed the sorrow and pain she bottled up inside. When she finished, the husband immediately knelt down and repented before the Lord for his failures as a husband, father, and man of God. The wife then followed her husband's example. The result was a transformed relationship between husband and wife as well as with God.

Repentance isn't only for new converts. Once a person becomes a Christian, that person can't set repentance aside and go merrily on their way. Even the most seasoned Christian needs to take a moral and spiritual inventory and repent in areas where they discover weakness. We must heed Romans 6:12, "Therefore do not let sin reign in our mortal body so that you obey its evil desires."

God calls each to repentance and doesn't know a better time to repent then right now. God's grace reaches beyond guilt and shame and bridges the gap between Him and us. He doesn't condemn our failures. He desires a continual relationship with us. However, without repentance, the sin we trifle with, make excuses for, or attempt to justify separates us from both God and others.

Paul writes in Hebrews 12:1, "Therefore, since we are surrounded by such a great cloud of witnesses, let us throw off everything that hinders and the sin that so easily entangles, and let us run with perseverance the race marked out for us."

How do you throw off what hinders you? How do you liberate yourself from the sin that so easily entangles you? If you've struggled for any length of time with a particular sin in your life, you realize you don't have power to overcome it. If you had had the power, you would've dealt with it a long time ago. So, what can you do? There's no easy solution, no formula I can share. We can't go into your basement or your garage, mix up a formula, and, when it's been mastered, put it to work in life. And, once it's been activated, suddenly we're free. Very few things work this way. Repentance may seem simple, but heartfelt repentance isn't always easy. It's releasing something we want that keeps us from what God has for us. We're heading in a certain direction and we're instructed it's the wrong way, so we turn around.

Hebrews 12:2 states, "Let us fix our eyes on Jesus, the author and perfecter of our faith…" We can't do this alone. We need both Jesus and the work of the Holy Spirit. When we're actively walking with Christ, we're striving to live our lives to please God. The Holy Spirit is also actively moving to guide us into all truth. And, when He illuminates an area of our life, a behavior, an attitude, or a thought that's not pleasing to Him or in line with His purpose, we should repent.

I believe many of us could pause right now and write down those areas in our life that hinder or entangle us. Do you already know the one thing keeping you from receiving all God has for you? Do you know the one thing that hinders you? If you turned a corner and came face-to-face with this thing, could you name it now? Many of us could put our finger on it within seconds.

Maybe it isn't a behavior or an attitude. Maybe God wants you to be more generous, but you refuse. God may want you to do something kind for someone who grates on your last nerve. When God asks me to do something and I either fail or refuse to act, that thing sits in my mind until I decide to step out in faith and do it. What is God asking of you right now?

The majority of us can pinpoint exactly what we've put off or failed to do, or what we shouldn't have done, and the thought processes we need to change. With that in mind, we have the opportunity to come to our senses. Hopefully, we don't find ourselves eating figurative pig slop. Hopefully, what comes to mind isn't as dramatic as Jim's situation. It doesn't matter what it is. If you're a prodigal or if you've been holding something back from God, it's time to come to your senses and repent. Now is the day. Now is the time. Don't delay.

If you're unsure of how to proceed, I encourage you to find Godly counsel; your pastor, a respected brother or sister in the Lord, or a leader you trust and respect. Find someone you're sure will be able to give good direction and advice. If you're facing something traumatic, find a safe environment in which to share it. Ask the Holy Spirit to guide and help you make a wise decision.

We've learned two truths from Jim. Here is where we find acceptance. First, God doesn't know a sin He won't forgive. No matter what you've done, no matter what kind of life you've lived. God is waiting for you. He loves you. His compassion and forgiveness are all-encompassing. The second truth is: God doesn't know a better time to repent. When we realize we've done wrong, when we sin, and it's time to turn from it, and change this truth reveals itself. When we realize we're away from God and that it's our sin which separates us from Him, if we want His forgiveness, we must repent. There's no better time than right now. Jim came to his senses and it led him back home.

Jim is about to embark on the journey to know the third truth and it's one he doesn't expect.

Chapter Twelve:

God Doesn't Know a Repentant Sinner Who Isn't Welcome

Jim took the long walk home after living in a distant land where even the pig slop looked good to him. He came to his senses and decided it couldn't be any worse back home. In fact, he knew it had to be better. After all, his father's servants had enough to eat. Even though he was unsure of the greeting awaiting him, he knew the answer deep in his spirit. When compared with how he was being treated at his current place of so-called employment, he knew it was better on his father's farm. For Jim, there was no doubt things were better at home. When he arrived exhausted, filthy, and apologetic, he discovered it was going to be far better than he expected.

The first truth, God doesn't know a sin He won't forgive, is always working in the background. That truth becomes evident when a person comes to his senses and embraces the second truth of repentance. Before Jim knew what was happening, he stepped from the second truth into the glorious sunshine of the first.

God doesn't know a better time to repent because He doesn't know a sin He won't forgive. There's no time gap. God never says, "Let them stew in their regret for awhile." Sometimes we expect God to punish us for our wrongs. It's a commonly held belief that God is just waiting to lower the boom on us.

Ralph was a friend from high school. As teenagers do, we played jokes on each other. After I played a good prank, Ralph would shake his finger at me and say, "God will get you for that." Granted, I think Ralph was only kidding. But his threat was a widespread belief. We may have joked about it, but one day God was going to "get me" for all the things I did wrong. This view of God is still common today. I've heard that if my rights outnumber my wrongs I'll be okay. However, the wrongs I've done will always outnumber those deeds I think I've done right. Even a lot of the things I did right were done for the wrong reason. My wrongful motivation offset any good I accomplished.

Because of God's grace, we receive what we don't deserve. God's forgiveness is always ready to burst into our lives as soon as we step into the second truth. It took Jim's step of faith to usher in the other truths. The nights Jim lay awake, full of remorse were not enough to invite God to enter his life. Jim could've cried himself to sleep each night, but the deepest level of sorrow wouldn't have been enough to bridge the gap between God and man. Jim could've decided to work harder to make up for his wrongdoing. He could've even become the finest man in the world. It wouldn't have been enough. He had to come to his senses, take the step of faith, and reach out to his father believing that his future was going to be better than his past.

I've met prodigals over the years who couldn't bring themselves to take that initial step. For whatever reason, they wouldn't accept that God's forgiveness was available. Some, with tears streaming down their face, would rebuff the invitation to pray for forgiveness. "No, it's too late." "I just can't do it." "I'm too far gone," they would say. Many had a deed they felt couldn't be forgiven and it blinded them to the first truth. We must take hold of the second truth in order to experience the first. Even if we don't know it, the first truth is always there. Even if we don't believe it, the first truth is always accurate. When we take one step into the second truth, God's forgiveness explodes into our heart, and it's then we begin to realize the third truth.

Jim's long journey back home led him to the third truth. This truth is simple, but is often the most difficult to comprehend. However, Jim ran headfirst into it.

God doesn't know a sin He won't forgive.

God doesn't know a better time to repent.

And, God doesn't know a repentant sinner, who isn't welcome.

On his homeward journey, Jim spent time rehearsing the speech to his father. I wonder how many renditions he went through? His painstaking search for the right word resulted in discarding one for another. Once he placed the new word in his speech, he paused, and started over. The sheer repetitiveness created ample frustration, depression, and self-loathing. Just as day ran into day, speech ran into speech. As Jim worked on the exact wording, I can picture him stopping on the side of the road and acting out the play as it unfolded in his mind. In the end, he'd kick a small stone or throw a stick in disgust. There wasn't a way to convey what he felt. How could he figure out what to say when he knew no words could ever explain his behavior or excuse the hurt and embarrassment he caused his family? No one knew that more than he did. He continued trying to come to the right conclusion, when no right conclusion could be found. The internal turmoil and struggle were too great.

We've all been in the same situation. When I was younger I couldn't seem to help myself. Given the opportunity, I'd do something wrong and soon I'd be standing in front of my parents, brothers, sisters, teachers, principle, or supervisor trying to explain my actions. I just couldn't seem to get it right. I often asked myself, "What's the use? Why would God want me?" I wonder how many times Jim wanted to turn around, ask for his old job back, and slop those hogs until he died? After all, he thought it was what he deserved.

I was about twenty-two and had been in the Air Force three years but hadn't made a 100 percent transition to military life. I still complained a lot about the military way of doing things. I hadn't embraced Uncle Sam's way of thinking. However, I'd recently received an early promotion called a "below-the-zone promotion" which served to push me into deciding I needed to become a more "responsible" Airman. Up to this point, I'd spent a significant amount of time goofing off and had earned a few minor infractions. But, after this promotion, I felt I needed to "shape up and fly right".

Our flight chief was a senior NCO who had his hands full with young Airmen. He not only had to deal with our off-duty stupidity, but also our tendency to be stupid while on duty. We'd been reminded countless times not to abuse the vehicles by speeding, off-roading, racing, and generally doing what young men do in vehicles they own as well as in those they don't. I'm not admitting anything, but does anyone realize the small Chevy S-10 government pickup truck can easily become airborne using a log and a three-quarter inch sheet of plywood as a take off ramp?

On Plattsburgh Air Force Base, the Weapons Storage Area, or WSA, had a section where bombs were stored in hardened bunkers called igloos. There were three rows with multiple igloos in each row. There was a paved road circling the three rows, with another road cutting through the center. This road provided access to the middle row. The front of each igloo had two solid steel doors fastened by a high-security padlock and a numeric seal. Each door also had an alarm system. This area was constantly patrolled by a two-man security team who provided a rapid response if an alarm was ever triggered without proper authentication.

Driving around this small area all night was more than a little boring. To relieve the boredom, we would see how fast we could drive around the circle, attempting to break the unofficial record. On one particular night, I was the ranking member and decided I was going to be responsible and not exceed the 15-mph speed limit.

One of my fellow cops relentlessly encouraged me to try breaking the record one last time. He must have asked me at least three times before I finally agreed. With the pedal to the metal, I sped off into the night. I entered the second turn doing just over sixty miles-per-hour and promptly lost control nearly rolling my vehicle. I left 124 feet of skid marks on the road. Yes, 124 feet of skid marks in a 15 miles per hour zone. I couldn't hide those dark streaks on the pavement, so it was just a matter of time before trouble came knocking. It wasn't long before I was relieved of my post and stood before Master Sergeant Wildoner trying to answer the age-old question that has no good explanation, "What in the world were you thinking?" I had to stand in front of a person of authority to give an account of my actions. I stood there trying to explain my actions but anything I said rang hollow. I was very fortunate my little trip around the WSA igloos didn't have lasting consequences.

Some are not that lucky. Remorse was Jim's constant companion. Regret was an unkind friend who greeted him every morning and was the last one he spoke to when he fell asleep. He visited with misery each workday. These non-friends traveled with him on the way home but offered no comfort. Jim needed to face the authority figure in his life. He had to face the man who taught him how to work, how to be an honorable person, and how to respect the family name. Jim didn't have a single good excuse. He was an outcast, a wretch, a sinner, a dishonor to his family and to his father. But, onward he walked.

In the story of the Prodigal Son, we need to turn our eyes to the last part of verse twenty and continue through verse twenty-two, "...he ran to his son, threw his arms around him and kissed him. The son said to him, 'Father, I have sinned against Heaven and against you. I am no longer worthy to be called your son.' But the father said to his servants, 'Quick! Bring the best robe and put it on him. Put a ring on his finger and sandals on his feet'."

Jim's father was watching for him and upon seeing him couldn't wait any longer. He ran to him. His embrace said it all. He was overwhelmed that his son was home and welcomed him without reservation.

When Jim was embraced by his father he said, "Father, I have sinned against Heaven and against you. I am no longer worthy to be called your son." But it seems the father was completely oblivious to his son's rehearsed speech. Instead of having to beg for forgiveness, Jim was greeted with a hug and a kiss.

At first, Jim was confused and didn't comprehend what was happening. Jim had just run headlong into the third truth, God doesn't know a sinner who repents who isn't welcome.

Jim was welcomed because he was redeemed. When you're redeemed, all your wrongs are gone. They vanish in an instant. Like Jim, we can't comprehend what happened. We believe we're going to be punished. We expect the punishment we think we deserve but get something unexpected instead. One day Jim doesn't think reconciliation is possible. He's alienated from his father. The next moment, he's completely accepted and welcomed with a party. This can be hard for us to accept. We know what we are. We know what we did. We know the pain it caused.

When I think about some of the things I've done over the years that no one else knows or when I look inward and see these deeds and my darkest desires, I reflect on not only what I could be but also what I'm capable of. We can all take this inward look with the same results. When we examine ourselves, we see our true condition and, one day, each of us will be called to give an account. On that day we'll bring all of it. When we stand before the highest Authority we know we're guilty and expect the axe to fall. But since we experienced the first two truths, we're welcomed without reservation, with overwhelming love, and celebration. Romans 5:8 explains the reason, "But God demonstrates His own love for us in this: While we were still sinners, Christ died for us."

The simple truth is the Father loves us. We couldn't do anything to deserve His love. Before we knew we needed our Father's love, He already took the necessary steps to ensure we had a way home. If Jim had tried to earn his father's acceptance, he would never have succeeded.

When my dad looked at me, he didn't see the things I'd done wrong. He saw me, his son. My children are now grown. When we moved to a new assignment, my adult children stayed behind or moved elsewhere. They started to live on their own and would agree their lives didn't go quite as planned. They made mistakes. However, when I look at them, I'm not reminded of all their mistakes. I'm excited to be able to see them. I'm filled with love and am overjoyed to embrace them because of love. They don't have to earn my love, because that's impossible. It's already been provided because they're in my family.

Steve, my friend from Plattsburgh, had a way of confronting me with truth. Once I was feeling I hadn't lived up to my potential. I felt conviction of some sin in my life. I had repented, but still felt troubled and told Steve about my struggle. He asked, "Are you righteous?"

My reply sounded defeated, "No, I don't feel that way."

He stepped up to me and stated with a certain amount of authority, "I didn't ask you how you feel. Are you righteous? Do you have right standing before God?"

His point was clear. I wasn't righteous because of anything I did or didn't do or because I decided I felt that way. I was righteous because I had right standing before God. Jesus's atoning sacrifice on the Cross provides all I need. His sacrifice is a way to be adopted into God's family, thereby obtaining right standing before God. Jim is like each person who experiences redemption. It's a wonderful, exciting experience you never expect. Jim didn't have time to give his speech nor make himself presentable. His father wasn't concerned about those things. He was concerned with only one thing, his son was home. When a sinner repents he's welcomed. It's just like coming home.

I previously explained how my uncle, a Baptist minister from Ohio, and his family came to visit my family in Rhode Island. On Sunday, he suggested we attend a Baptist church meeting in the local junior high school auditorium. Even after my uncle and his family left, we continued to attend. Shortly after we began attending, Pastor Rod started coming to our house for Monday night Bible studies. On these nights, if you were home, you attended the Bible study. I missed the first few Mondays while camping with my Boy Scout troop. On the third Monday in August, with all my camping trips completed, I attended my first home Bible study.

When I was a teenager, our little house in West Warwick, Rhode Island was nothing special. The front door opened into a small living room. When you entered, stairs leading to the second-floor bedrooms were directly in front of the door. The living room was two or three steps to the left. During the Bible study, the entire family sat in the living room.

After the study, everyone went either into the kitchen or upstairs to their rooms. Pastor Rod asked if he could talk to me for a moment, then walked me through the Gospel message and explained the plan of Salvation. That was the first time I remember clearly hearing the message of the Cross. When he finished, Pastor Rod asked if I wanted to pray and ask Christ into my life. I said I would. When I prayed on the living room couch long ago, it became an altar of prayer.

All these years later, two things remain clear. My first memory is of a slip of paper. When Pastor Rod explained the Gospel message, he used diagrams and phrases on a slip of paper to explain how I was lost and needed a Savior. When Pastor Rod, sitting next to me, invited me to pray, I told him I didn't know how or what to say. Up to this point, the only prayers I knew were "religious" prayers. Religious prayers aren't personal and heartfelt; when you pray these kinds of prayers, you often simply go through the motions, reciting words. We don't realize how powerful a righteous prayer can be and what it can accomplish. Since I'd never truly prayed before, I didn't know how to address the God of the Universe. It might seem odd, but looking back, it felt impossible that He, the Big Man upstairs, would listen to me. Doesn't it seem a little presumptuous that God, the Creator of the Universe, the all-powerful Maker of Heaven and Earth would stop running the cosmos and listen to what I had to say? I may have been a teenager, but I was suddenly aware I was a sinner and my sin was evident to God. It scared me and I didn't have a clue how to begin this prayer.

After that admission, Pastor Rod put his hand on my shoulder and said it was okay. He handed me the slip of paper and suggested I might find it useful as a guide. I remember looking down at the paper with its simple drawings and Bible verses. Some words were written sideways and the pictures weren't drawn by a professional artist, but they made it clear how the whole thing worked.

I doubt my prayer was elegant or insightful. I'm sure I wasn't able to clearly convey the step of faith I was taking. I had no idea how expressing a need for forgiveness and inviting Jesus into my life to save me would impact my life. But, I looked at that little slip of paper in my trembling fingers and fumbled through some sort of prayer. When I was done, I looked up and said, "I think that's it."

Pastor Rod patted me on the back and replied, "Amen. You are now a Christian."

That was how my spiritual journey started. I didn't do anything to earn it. I just accepted it. As a young man of fifteen, I was aware of my sin and knew I needed a Savior. As soon as I heard the Gospel message, I came to my senses and took the first step home.

The second thing I remember still amazes me. If my prayer had been recorded, no one would say it should have been archived as one of the greatest prayers ever spoken. And if we heard the recording today, I'm sure I'd be embarrassed by the stammering, pausing, and fumbling. Although my first prayer wasn't worth remembering, it was the most important prayer of my life. That prayer did everything it was supposed to.

When Pastor Rod patted me on the back and said "Amen,"

we walked into the kitchen where he then announced, "We have a new Christian in the house."

I don't remember anyone's reaction or what was said. What I do recall is when I walked away from that couch, I felt lighter, different. I didn't understand it, but I knew I was changed. I know now that the difference was the first and second truths we've already covered. When I took the step of repentance, God's forgiveness rushed into my life and changed me. I was spiritually different and felt that change physically as well.

The third truth soon began to reveal itself. I, who was previously separated from God, was now accepted. I was accepted completely, wholly, and without reservation. My sins were gone and I not only felt different, I was different. That change made me acceptable to God and I now had a personal relationship with Him. This relationship would change everything.

Over the next few years I learned the depth of this change and how it should impact my relationships. Some friends no longer accepted me. At first, they questioned if what I was talking about was real, but soon didn't want anything to do with me. But, I found this new faith opened doors to other relationships I never expected.

I believe faith in Christ transcends our history or race as well as our economic past and future. All are welcomed. Faith in Christ challenges us to see things through God's eyes not through the veils of our bias and prejudice. I found not only was I welcomed into God's kingdom, but also didn't have to wait to be accepted into His kingdom on earth. I found brothers and sisters in Faith are not limited to my race, economic background, or the area in which I grew up.

The same night I prayed in the living room in our little house, I discovered the third truth: God doesn't know a repentant sinner who isn't welcomed. Not only did God forgive all my sin as soon as I repented, but He also welcomed me into a family I never knew existed. God will never leave me and is always with me. He provides comfort and guidance when I ask, but His provision doesn't stop there.

One of my first after-school jobs was working at the Beacon gas station at the end of Tollgate Road. In those days, very few gas stations were self-serve. The cost of a gallon of gas hovered around 55 cents. We not only filled the cars with gas, we also checked the oil, washed windows, and even put air in the tires.

One summer day a car with Minnesota license plates pulled in for a fill-up. As I was putting gas in his car, the driver got out. "You're a long way from home," I commented.

"This is home now," he replied. "I'm the new pastor at the church on Bald Hill Road."

My face lit up as I explained, "I'm a Christian."

A month or two previously the little Baptist church I attended closed and Pastor Rod moved to a new church in Kansas. I wondered where I'd attend church. Enter a car from Minnesota. Pastor Pender invited me to visit any time.

On a Wednesday evening, when my gas station shift ended I hurried to make it to Bible study at the church on Bald Hill Road. I hadn't had time to change my clothes or wash my stained hands, I went just as I was. Pastor Pender welcomed me dirt and all. The little white church on Bald Hill Road soon became my family's home church. When you are welcomed by God, your family suddenly gets larger too.

When we're welcomed into God's Kingdom, we experience redemption. We're welcomed home without reservation. All our wrongs are gone. Our past lives and our old stories are rewritten without the tragic ending. We show up in our deplorable condition and expect punishment but are greeted with love and acceptance. Our old, soiled clothes are removed and we're given the best robe. We're changed and no longer look as we did moments before. The rough and rocky roads have taken a toll on our feet, but we now wear new sandals that transform us from slave to family member. A ring placed on our finger gives us status. It shows to whom we belong. I'm now accepted. I was a wretch but after repentance I stand before God righteous, justified, and forgiven. Once you experience redemption, you'll know you've been changed.

My friend Bob described how he experienced redemption. He stated that when he rose the next morning, "The grass looked greener. The trees were fuller and the birds' songs sounded sweeter. Even work looked better."

What made such a difference? He was redeemed. Not only was he welcomed by God, but he was also welcomed into the family of God. His sin was gone and he knew something had changed within him. It reminds me of a song by Tim Hughes, an ordained minister in the Church of England. Tim recorded this song in September of 2008, in London. The chorus of his song, "Happy Day," goes like this:

> *Oh, Happy Day, Happy Day*
> *You washed my sin away*
> *Oh, Happy Day, Happy Day*
> *I'll never be the same*
> *Forever I am changed* [10]

We're welcomed without reservation, without hesitation, and without pause. When we take the initial step of repentance, we experience God's forgiveness, and suddenly we're ushered into a relationship we never expected.

Mike is one of my brother's in the Lord. He worked for me for a few years in the Air Force before accepting an opportunity to change his military specialty. Mike was originally an Air Force Supply Sergeant, but after a few years, he applied and was accepted to work in the chapel. After a few years, he again applied and was accepted for a new specialty in the missile fields of Wyoming. Mike and his wife were both prodigals. Mike was raised in church but had drifted away. I'm not aware of his wife's spiritual background, but she was in a similar condition. As their family prepared for the move to Wyoming, Mike and his wife decided to separate. Even when he moved away, Mike and I occasionally kept in touch.

Flash forward ten years. I arrived at my new duty station, Scott Air Force Base, Illinois just east of St. Louis. Who did I run into? Mike and his family, who are now together and whole again. One day, as we were talking, I asked how it happened. Just like Jim, everyone has a story and I love to hear a person's story. Mike's wife told of the heartache and difficulty they faced being apart and trying to raise children. They decided to give their marriage another try.

She tells the story this way: "One Easter morning, I suggested maybe we should go to church. Mike selected a familiar church name, we got ready, packed up the family, and off we went. As we were sitting in church, suddenly it all made sense and when the altar call was given, I answered." Mike followed his wife's example a couple of weeks later and repented. Suddenly, all things changed in their lives and they were welcomed into the family of God. It all made sense and the prodigals came home.

Sometimes when we review the choices we've made our lives seem hopeless. We've been told all our lives God is angry and will punish us. That was probably Jim's thought. Even as a fifteen-year-old boy I questioned how I could ever be accepted. Not only are we accepted, we are welcomed. It all makes sense.

But there is more. There's one additional truth God doesn't know and it's profound.

This is what we've learned thus far:

God doesn't know a sin He won't forgive.

God doesn't know a better time to repent.

And, God doesn't know a repentant sinner, who isn't welcomed.

What's the fourth truth we must learn? God doesn't know a life that can't be renewed.

Chapter Thirteen:

God Doesn't Know a Life That Can't Be Renewed

One nice thing about the military is you often cross paths with people years after your initial meeting. Fred was one friend I had the privilege of serving with at two different locations. Fred was a bit of a loner. He didn't like large groups but was easy to talk to and liked to play cards, especially Spades.

I first met Fred in the United Kingdom. While in England, Fred had no interest in spiritual matters. He wasn't mean, but clearly stated he didn't understand all the "religious stuff" and wasn't interested. Fred was a prodigal and felt no need to change. We still became good friends and saw each other on a weekly basis. It was good to pause and spend some time talking. I left our base in the United Kingdom and with this permanent change of station, Fred and I parted company. I didn't expect to see him again.

I'd been at my new assignment for over a year before I ran into Fred. When you run into someone you haven't seen in a long while the conversation goes something like this: "Hey, look who it is." "It's so good to see you." "When did you get here?" It only takes about half an hour to get caught up.

Fred and I got together for dinner several times. I showed him my favorite fishing spots, and we did a little camping. One night we'd gone to dinner and were driving back to base when the conversation turned to God. Fred was more open and had many questions about what faith requires and what the Bible says about certain subjects.

I soon felt the need to pull over in order to could give the conversation my undivided attention. After we passed through the base's main gate, I parked at the recreation center. The conversation continued for a long time. With more and more questions being answered, Fred was running out of excurses and God was about to burst into his life. We began discussing the plan of salvation and the conversation flowed as naturally as a mountain stream.

"Did you want to pray and invite Christ into your life?" I asked.

"Yes," was his sincere response. As soon as we started praying, Fred began to cry. The emotional reaction completely surprised him. He looked at me and said, "Why did it take so long? I feel totally new."

The three previous truths culminate in the fourth, making the others all worthwhile but it's also the hardest to fully grasp. Although Fred was at the start of a journey he expressed the truth perfectly. "I feel totally new."

God does not know a sin He won't forgive.

God does not know a better time to repent.

God does not know a repentant sinner, who isn't welcome.

God also, does not know a life that can't be renewed.

The first three truths are part of Jim's story. They're part of all our stories. No matter where you are in life's journey, you see yourself somewhere on the path Jim walked. If I pause long enough, I can see myself at the different intersections where Jim found himself.

When someone comes to the Cross and accepts Christ as his Lord and Savior, that person officially gets to start life anew. We get off the couch and feel different, we shed tears of redemption in a car, or find ourselves in any other place, and at that moment, at that place, life begins fresh and new. We'll still have issues for God to work on, but no matter what our condition we've just been reborn. This truth impacts every new believer, because no matter how broken the life, God doesn't know a life that can't be made new.

The most fascinating part of Jim's story is the end because of the unknown element. We know Jim came to his senses and made the journey home. We know his father welcomed him with clearly expressed emotion. We also know he was welcomed home with new raiment, shoes, the family ring, and a celebration. What we don't know is what happened to Jim afterward.

Everything Jim learned on the road of life didn't prepare him for his next step. Jim could have returned home and picked up where he left off. When the party was over, what would Jim feel? How would he behave? Now Jim would have to deal with what happens after conversion.

He learned many significant life lessons on his road trip. I'm sure he appreciated his father more. He appreciated a filling meal and a refreshing shower followed by clean clothes. However, his appreciation doesn't signify he was changed. He could have felt privileged and entitled which would negate all he learned on his trip. What really needed to change was Jim's heart. Without an inward change, Jim was still the same old person. Just like Jim, unless our heart changes, we'll remain the poor wretch we've always been. Only God can change a person's heart.

This is one of the greatest truths found in Scripture. When we realize we're a wretch and decide to return to the Father, we each experience everything Jim did. But, our acceptance doesn't stop there. God changes us on the inside which ultimately creates change on the outside. There is no greater change I've seen than when a person meets Jesus in a very personal way.

My buddy Steve, from Plattsburgh, changed seemingly overnight. Another man stationed with us said, "It was like flipping a light switch." With one flick of the switch he was different. The only explanation Steve could give was that he was changed on the inside. His life was renewed and he was able to start again. To use a biblical term, you could say those who experience this life changing relationship in God are "born again." They discover they both feel and actually are totally new.

I've had people point out we really don't know how the story ends and I won't argue. We know the most important lessons Jim learned when he arrived home were his father's unconditional love, forgiveness, and acceptance. After facing our first three truths, Jim is then confronted with the fourth; God doesn't know a life that can't be renewed. The story Jesus told ends at the party. But, that isn't where the story truly ends.

The personal stories I've retold in the previous pages are all the same. We don't know how they end. I'm still connected in various ways with a few people who've crossed my path. Some I haven't seen for years. Others I've recently connected with through social media. In spite of that, I still can't answer the question, "How did their stories unfold?" For most, the story's ending will remain unknown on this side of Heaven.

When convicted of sin, some may be like me and refuse to

accept the work God wants to do in us. When I was in my early twenties, I too had an angry attitude. To be accurate, I had deep-rooted anger issues. I felt convicted of sin, but I refused to deal with my anger. The result was I walked away from God for a season. After years of following Christ, I became a prodigal until, just like Jim, I came to my senses and returned to the Father. Even though I'd already experienced the first three truths and willingly walked away, as soon as I came to my senses I relived them all. Then I was ready to embrace the fourth. Submitting to God, I allowed Him to renew me, cleanse me from the sin of anger, and develop a new perspective without the excess baggage.

Let's walk with Jim a little further and pick up his story after the party. What will we find? I imagine Jim was truly changed by his experience. When we met Jim in the first chapter, he described moving from death to life. Before deciding to return home, he was dead. But, after experiencing his father's unconditional love, forgiveness, and acceptance his life was renewed.

I've had people tell me Jim's real-life experiences would have changed him. I'm not so sure. I've known far too many for whom this truth doesn't apply. It's possible Jim was different because of what he'd experienced. But, it's also possible that in spite of them he remained the same. Or, worse yet, it's possible he was even worse than before. Not everyone who experiences either hardships or blessings changes for the better. I'm not focused on those changes caused when Jim was forced to end his wild living because he was penniless. Nor, the changes he promised to make out of regret because he remembered the shame he brought to the family or the hurtful things said on his way out the door. The changes I speak of weren't encountered on his road trip. They center on his confrontation with the first three truths; those profound changes we only experience after coming face-to-face with the living God.

When Jim left home he was a mess. When he returned he was a mess. The difference between the two is that when Jim left, he didn't realize he was a mess. When he returned, he now knew what everyone else already knew, he was wretched. Before he left, he displayed pride and arrogance he couldn't hide. He was disobedient and disrespectful in his dealings with others. Everyone knew how Jim behaved. His obnoxious attitude defined him and if someone didn't like it, he didn't care.

For a period of time in the city, this personality continued to serve him well. When you're funding the party, people tolerate a lot. However, when the money ran out, his antics were no longer amusing. It didn't take long for Jim to learn what everyone already knew. Nobody really liked him. By the time he set out for home, his outward appearance reflected his inward reality. But, his story doesn't end there.

When Jim came face-to-face with his father's acceptance, he had some decisions to make. He could remain the same or he could change. He could pick up where he left off or put his father's grace to work in himself. What if he was overwhelmed by his father's unconditional acceptance and decided his greatest joy would be to please his father? What if he suddenly saw the potential within and freely accepted the guidance necessary to bring that potential to the surface? What if he didn't see his own potential, but because his father believed in him, he stretched and learned in order to meet his father's requests. What if he chose to put his father's love into practice? Jim appeared with new garments and a ring, but also had a changed heart that reflected his father's love. He was changed on the inside.

That's exactly what the Heavenly Father's grace does. We all have the opportunity to experience God's forgiveness. When we're confronted by our sin and repent, we're flooded by God's amazing grace. We don't deserve it, but if we accept, we reap the benefits of His forgiveness. When we're confronted by God's love we must decide whether or not we're going to repent and accept it. When God offers His forgiveness, we have a decision to make. If we accept, we step into a whole new world and experience exactly what Jim experienced, our Father's grace.

As I mentioned previously, the point behind grace is we receive what we don't deserve. We can never balance the scales between good deeds and bad. Recently I watched a preacher demonstrate grace. He walked five or six feet down the church's center aisle and stopped. The third person in the row was a young lady. He asked her name and handed her a one hundred-dollar bill before returning to the pulpit. She'd done nothing to deserve such a gift. However, she willingly accepted it as a gift. This simple example provides a demonstration of God's grace. We don't do anything to deserve it. We just accept it.

If embracing his life experiences was all Jim did, he wouldn't be any better on the inside. What's the overall difference if Jim stayed the same inside? What if there was no change to his heart? What good would it do if he cleaned up on the outside but stayed the same on the inside?

As I explained earlier, everyone faces the struggle for acceptance. Until we truly find what we're seeking, it never disappears. When we realize forgiveness is available and repent, we're accepted into the Father's house. Our heart is changed.

Here's the power of salvation. It isn't only a change in perspective. It isn't just a different point of view. We become a new creation. We're a whole new person. When you accept Jesus, when you realize God did everything and you did nothing, everything in your life changes. Then, the portion of the story we don't know begins.

Change is difficult and never a smooth road. Jim's journey would initially have been a rocky one. There would be days when his old attitude would resurface. There would be occasions when he didn't understand why he was assigned a task. There would be instances where he'd be angry. But, the beginning of the journey isn't an indication of how it ends. The Father loves us enough to ensure we are led straight into our fourth and final truth.

God does not know a life that can't be renewed.

When Jim came home he was wounded but his life was a reflection of the number of bad choices he made. His was a long journey and I'm sure he had to face a certain amount of ridicule and abuse while on the road. But, his story wasn't one that could be kept hidden in his small town where he was certain to face additional derision. Jim had been a mess on the inside for years, but now it was clear he was a mess on the outside as well. When Jim experienced his father's unconditional love, his complete acceptance, and his uncompromising forgiveness he participated in one of the most amazing acts of God when He changes those who come to Him.

When a person comes to the Cross and repents of his sin, God doesn't leave him neck-deep in his mess. He begins a work that completely changes the person's life and condition. It doesn't happen overnight. It's a lifelong journey of transformation.

Second Corinthians 5:17 tells us, "I am a new creation, the old is gone the new has come."

When we take the step and ask for forgiveness, God shows us His forgiveness was available all the time. He welcomes us home and throws us a party, but one of the greatest gifts is that He doesn't stop there. He doesn't merely change our appearance, He changes our hearts and way of thinking.

Every life given to God is redeemable. No matter how bad,

every life can be transformed. That's because God doesn't know a life that can't be renewed. We're all rebellious. We're in the same shape when we call out to the Father, "I am a wretch. I am a sinner in need of a Savior." In lives marked by sin, pain, and suffering we all walk along and, just like Jim, we're really the walking wounded. Some wounds are made by our choices, some by the choices of others. The end result is the same, we're all sinners in need of a Savior. Our lives need renewal. When we stand at the foot of the Cross, we stand as equals. All we have to offer are our broken and wounded lives. Because of His love, He takes that life, molds it, shapes it, and transforms it. God reveals our hidden potential and takes us places we never dreamed possible.

Psalms 40:2-3 states, "He brought me out of the pit, out of the miry clay. He established my goings and He put a new song in my mouth."

It may be enough to know we'll be welcomed home and a celebration hosted in our honor. It may be enough to know that after our wanderings and sullied lives, the past will be forgiven and forgotten. But, the work isn't done. God loves us far too much to leave us in that condition. When Jesus told this parable, He didn't tell us how it ends. Jim's story doesn't end with the party. As is true for Jim, our journeys, our stories are just beginning.

For the most part, I don't know what happened to the people whose paths I've crossed after moving to a new assignment. Many, I'm sure, have experienced pain, disappointment, and heartache as well as other burdens they carry to this day. Their stories aren't finished either. Scripture tells me I can have confidence "… because I know whom I have believed, and am convinced that He is able to guard what I have entrusted to Him until that day" (2 Timothy 1:12).

If…I believe God can forgive all my sin, I can also believe He will hear me when I repent. And if He hears me when I repent, I can also believe God will welcome me into His family. Then, I can certainly trust Him to take what's left of my life and transform, renew, and change it.

In my own life, I experienced more heartache than I want to remember. Trouble and pain have been constant passengers alongside me as I've traveled this life. Occasionally one of these passengers will disappear, but I know he'll be back. He always seems to return.

Despite pain, suffering, disappointment, and struggle, the fourth truth is still evident. It's still true. God doesn't know a life that can't be renewed. I not only experienced it when I first came to Him, but also each time I return to Him in repentance. When I'm feeling defeated, tired, and hopeless, I know God can restore my soul. God is constantly calling us to renewal even when we're already walking by His side.

On one assignment, I particularly remember a late night at work. I was desperately trying to meet an unrealistic deadline set by someone higher in the chain of command. This, along with some of the struggles I was experiencing at home, made me both exhausted and frustrated. To top it off, the data for the report didn't meet the minimum criteria and I couldn't find the correct information. Although it seemed serious then, I have no memory of what the report was about or why it was regarded as important.

However, I promised my boss I'd finish it and he was counting on me. There were times while trying to achieve those lofty goals I became weary, irritated, and annoyed. This was one of those times. My condition that night was not positive. I was tired of the ongoing disagreements at home and the difficulties at work, but all that's unimportant. What's important is the lesson I was about to receive on the fourth truth. God's renewal is always available to us and, if we're willing to yield, He doesn't hesitate to provide it.

I had some music playing in the background and, as one song started, I felt the Spirit of the Lord tug on my heart telling me to pause. At first, I resisted. I needed to get that report done. But the calling persisted and before the song ended I did stop to listen. The song was nearly over but I got quiet. This is what I heard:

Take My yoke upon you and walk here by My side
Let Me heal your heartaches, dry the tears you've cried
Never will I leave you, never turn away
Keep you through the darkness lead you through the day
If you're tired and weary, weak and heavy laden
I can understand how it feels to be alone
I will take your burden, if you'll let Me love you,
Wrap My arms around you, Give your heart a home [11]

I not only paused, I also stopped to rewind the tape. The song spoke of hollow laughter and secret pain each of us has if we have difficulties with work, home, marriage, kids, health, or life. I had each of those and was tired of the fight. Life requires us to be resilient, but what do you do when you're "tired and weary"? What do you do when you don't have much hope? I found the answer, when I stopped and listened to a song.

As I listened to the song, both my night and my next day were transformed. I spent some time in worship while this song played and allowed the Holy Spirit to minister to me. The report, due first thing in the morning, would have to wait. I played that song over and over and God's renewal washed over me. Soon I was refreshed. My mind and attitude were clear. I did finish the report and went home in a much better condition than when I'd arrived at my office. The circumstances at work hadn't changed.

The circumstances at home hadn't either. But I felt empowered to face the trials in my life and try again. I was renewed.

This event made it clear that when I'm overwhelmed by life's events if I pause and spend some time with my Lord, He renews my spirit. He gives me strength when I'm weak. He gives me hope for tomorrow. The journey continues when the alarm goes off in the morning and we'll all face sorrow, death, and difficulties. But God promises to renew us. If you feel tired, weak, and burdened by life's heavy load that you carry each day, it doesn't have to end there. The Lord understands and is ready to renew your strength and hope.

Not only has God forgiven me, welcomed me into His family, and renewed my life, He also does it continuously.

Each of these truths applies to new believers as well as those who've been walking in faith for many years. When I came to Christ at fifteen, I experienced all four truths. Now after following Jesus all these years, I still need to experience them regularly.

CHAPTER FOURTEEN:

WHAT'S NEXT?

In a short span of time, we've covered four truths revealed by the parable of the Prodigal Son.

God doesn't know a sin He won't forgive.

God doesn't know a better time to repent.

God doesn't know a repentant sinner, who isn't welcome.

God doesn't know a life that can't be renewed.

The last question is: Where do we go from here? These four truths require action on our part. We need to apply what Jim learned in order to impact our lives today.

Each of the four truths can be applied to our lives. What Jim learned and experienced is just as relevant today as it was when Jesus told the story. In order to answer the question, we need to pause and examine our own lives and where we stand in our relationship with God.

What kind of prodigal are you? Do you have a personal relationship with Jesus Christ? Do you know what I mean by that? I'm not asking if you know about Jesus. I'm not asking if you know the Bible. I'm not asking if you believe in God. I'm asking whether or not you have a living relationship with the Creator of the Universe. Have you accepted Jesus as your Lord and Savior?

I recently had a sad conversation with a woman who was raised in the church. She clearly knew the Scriptures and what God required. She comprehended her spiritual needs and how, when they're neglected, they negatively impact her physical, mental, and financial needs. In turn her health suffered. Disregard for her spiritual condition led to her moral breakdown as well as a host of other problems. She accepted the consequences of the life choices and voluntarily admitted her abandonment of her relationship with Jesus began her downfall. She said the neglect started slowly and went unnoticed. With each passing day, priorities changed and habits, once held dear, were no longer viewed as important or even relevant. Friends drifted away and their replacements didn't honor her friendship and trust. In time, she exchanged her strong, sure values for weaker ones.

As we talked, she related many heartaches and poor choices that brought unimaginable consequences. She said, "Looking back, I can see how I got here. But, when it came time to pay the piper, I was still surprised when he knocked on the door. The payment he wanted was expensive." She expressed regrets, for the pain she'd caused her family and for the heartache of being an outsider in the eyes of her loved ones. During these confessions, there were no tears, no heavy emotional sighs, and no angry outbursts. I listened to the many stories that twisted a cruel heaviness over our spirits and turned a sunny day into a melancholy afternoon. Ultimately, she shrugged her shoulders and said, "I guess this is just the way it is."

That doesn't have to be the way it is. Each of us has the opportunity to accept these truths and experience what Jim did long ago. Jesus calls each of us to experience God's forgiveness and redemption on a deeply personal level. Each of these truths is vital to our mental, physical, and spiritual well-being.

Several years ago Steve, my friend from Plattsburgh, learned he had cancer. He told me a story that made him smile. One day, he was sitting in the oncologist's office waiting for his turn to take his "poison", which was what he called his chemotherapy. He and another man were watching a "dumb daytime television show". Steve turned and said, "Hey, where you gonna be in 10,000 years?" He told me the guy looked at him as if he was crazy. But, Steve was serious, and he pressed on to discuss God's forgiveness and His love for us.

So, I'll ask you. Where will you be in 10,000 years? Can you tell me why God would let you into Heaven? Why would God forgive your sin and bring you from death into life?

No one is good enough to merit God's forgiveness. We can't earn our way to Heaven, no matter how many good deeds we've accomplished. Even if we have the purest intentions, we'll still fall short. It only took one sin for us to be separated from God and most of us can honestly account for far more than one.

Our sins require a perfect payment. That's the whole purpose of Jesus's mission to earth. He was born to be our payment. His death, burial, and resurrection paved the way for our redemption. He freely offers His forgiveness. All you need to do is ask.

It isn't complicated. You don't need to recite a long, drawn-out prayer or have an extensive vocabulary. You simply need to realize you're a sinner and accept that Jesus Christ paid the debt for your sin. Believe in your heart that Jesus died for your sins and arose on the third day. Repent of your sin and make a profession of faith that Jesus is your Lord and Savior. The only thing that matters is that you pray from your heart and are sincere.

Here's an example of a sinner's prayer:

> "Dear Lord Jesus, I confess I'm a sinner. I realize
> I've sinned and need forgiveness. I repent of my
> sin. Please forgive me and come into my life. I
> accept you as my Lord and Savior. Amen."

Once you accept Jesus, a transformation begins. The Holy Spirit begins His work to clean you from the inside. Although your prayer may be different from the example, the simple prayer you pray, starts your remarkable journey.

As soon as you pray, the four truths flood your life. They don't wait to see how the story ends. They permeate your soul and begin the work you've put off for far too long.

After spending some time thinking of the first truth that God doesn't know a sin He won't forgive, you realize God can forgive everyone because that's His nature. He wipes the slate clean and you are now born again.

Don't wait until you "fix" all that's wrong with you. If you could actually repair yourself, there would be no reason for Jesus's suffering and death. Repentance is the act of turning from your sin, rotating 180 degrees, and walking towards God. There's no reason to wait because God doesn't know a better time to repent.

Anyone who repents experiences the first two truths and is then confronted by the third when God welcomes you into His family. God doesn't know a repentant sinner who isn't welcomed with open arms.

People around you may behave differently. If you aren't used to the company of Christians, it may take some adjustment to this new life. A co-worker once came to church with me and when the minister gave an invitation for salvation, he went forward and accepted Jesus as his Savior. When everyone in this little church rejoiced, all he could say was, "This is a little strange if you ask me." He was welcomed into the family, but he was certainly not immediately comfortable.

Even if you're alone, the third truth is equally real. As soon as you repent, whether in or outside of church, in a group or alone, at home or in a distant land, it's all the same. The good news is God has forgiven you and now you're welcomed. You've experienced the third truth.

The fourth truth immediately begins to work. Your spiritual life has begun in earnest and you start growing. You'll find there's much to learn but God will guide you throughout the coming years. Just as when you were physically born, being spiritually born starts you on the journey to maturity. No matter your life condition, God is now working on your renewal. No matter your age or how serious your mistakes, God does not know a life that can't be renewed. We're broken but God knows how repair us.

I recently heard an old song by Daniel Amos. The song's chorus has the line, "And for Heaven's sake, someone take this aching away." [12] We've all experienced pain, heartache, regrets, and trauma in our relatively short lives. Although God can't change what you've experienced, He can begin the process of healing, renewal, and redemption.

You've been introduced to the four truths of what God doesn't know. If you prayed to accept Jesus into your life for the first time, let me be the first to say, "Welcome to the family." If you prayed to receive Jesus as Savior in the past, I welcome you home again. I encourage you to find a good, Bible-believing church. If you don't have a Bible, acquire one and start reading the New Testament. Get involved in a Bible study to help you learn about this new journey.

Some of us have followed Christ for years. We know the biblical truth of God's love and forgiveness. I've recounted my salvation experience from over forty years ago and many of you can do the same. You can state where you were, the time of day, and remember those who were with you. Be cautious not to take God's forgiveness for granted. He loves us with an everlasting love, but my hope is to never take it for granted as I have in the past.

I frequently need to pause and examine my life to ensure there isn't a secret sin taking root. I need to remember there are times when I need to repent from things that displease the Lord. I never want to become callous about God's ongoing work in my life. I need to always be sensitive to His work and, when He convicts me of sin, I take time to immediately repent. Yes, I mean immediately! Don't put it off, don't wait, do it now. Why? Although we know God doesn't know a sin He won't forgive, we also know there's no better time to repent than right now.

When I ask a group the simple question, "What's the one thing God is asking you to repent of?", without fail, individuals will rise from their seats, step out of the pews and come forward to pray. We're all works in progress and won't be perfect until we reach Heaven. We need to repent to keep the work of God fresh in our lives.

What does God want you to give Him? What habit do you need help to change? What's causing you to falter during your Christian journey? Don't let that sin remain. Take a moment to honestly examine your life and ask the Holy Spirit to reveal problem areas. Allow Him to help you grow and cleanse any sin in your life.

When I repent, I'm enveloped by God's love and grace. It feels as sweet as it did all those years ago. I never cease to be amazed by how much He loves me. However, there are times when I repent and don't feel any different. His love is true even when I don't feel it. The Creator of the Universe loves me on my best as well as my worst days, whether or not I feel differently. The truth is He loves me. That's amazing, but it gets even better. Even after I've experienced His love and acceptance, I still sometimes disappoint Him. And, He still loves me. He still accepts me. He still welcomes me. Even when I do something that's outside God's will, far from His best desire for my life, that I feel His displeasure, His love endures. When I measure myself in the light of His Word, I often find I miss the mark. But God, the Creator who knows everything about me, still welcomes me with open arms.

As God continues His work in me, I seek Him in prayer, in Bible reading, and in worship. During the hardest times, He wraps His arms around me and renews me. Even when my night is darkest, He gives renewed strength for another day.

No matter the condition. No matter the circumstance. No matter the difficulty. God renews me every morning and every night. When I reach out, He empowers me to walk the path ahead. The same promises He's given me, He's also given you.

The four truths I've described are simple. They aren't necessarily deep theological truths scholars ponder, discuss, or write about over hundreds of years. But, these truths were taught by Jesus in the Prodigal Son parable over 2,000 years ago and lay the foundation in a believer's life that will carry him all the way to the gates of Heaven.

Works Cited

1   All scripture quotations are taken from the Holy Bible, New International Version, published by Zondervan, 1984.

2   DeGarmo and Key, "All the Losers Win", *Mission of Mercy,* Power Discs, 1983.

3   DeGarmo and Key, "I'm Accepted", *The Pledge, Forefront Records,* 1989.

4   Lockyer, Herbert Sr., Nelson's Illustrated Bible Dictionary, Thomas Nelson Publishers, 1986, page 798.

5   Newton, John, "Amazing Grace", Book of Worship for United States Forces, US Government Printing Office, 1974

6   Divorce Statistics and Divorce Rate in USA, No date indicated. Retrieved from http://www.divorcestatistics.info/divorce-statistics-and-divorce-rate-in-the-usa.html

7   Barna, G., New Marriage and Divorce Statistics Released. March 31, 2008. Retrieved from https://www.barna.com/research/new-marriage-and-divorce-statistics-released/

8   ibid

9   Divorce Statistics and Divorce Rate in USA, No date indicated. Retrieved from http://www.divorcestatistics.info/divorce-statistics-and-divorce-rate-in-the-usa.html

10 Hughes, Tim, "Happy Day", *Holding Nothing Back,* Survivor Records, 2008

11 Francisco, Don, "Give Your Heart a Home", *The Traveler,* New Pax, 1981.

12 Daniel Amos, "Hound of Heaven", *Horrendous Disc,* Solid Rock, 1978

Printed in the United States
By Bookmasters